Reviewers

We would like to thank the following educators who reviewed, tested, or coordinating the reviewing of this series of GEMS materials in manuscript form. Their critical comments and recommendations contributed significantly to these GEMS publications. Their participation does not necessarily imply endorsement of the GEMS program.

Lynn Allen
Piedmont Middle School, Piedmont

Ann L. Babcock
Whatcom Middle School
Bellingham, WA

Karen Ginsberg Beroldo
St. Paul's Episcopal School, Oakland

Susan Butsch
Albany Middle School, Albany

David Collins
Bancroft Junior High School, San Leandro

Robin Davis
Albany Middle School, Albany

Marianne Gielow
Piedmont Middle School, Piedmont

Jaine Gilbert
Martin Luther King Junior High School, Berkeley

Catherine Heck
Bancroft Junior High School, San Leandro

Paul Mason Hynds
Bancroft Junior High School, San Leandro

*Kerri Lubin
Piedmont Middle School, Piedmont

Jack McFarland
Albany Middle School, Albany

Ann Mosle
Bancroft Junior High School, San Leandro

Joy Osborn
Columbus Intermediate School, Berkeley

Susan B. Porter
St. Paul's Episcopal School, Oakland

*Stephen Rutherford
Bancroft Middle School, San Leandro

Phoebe A. Tanner
Columbus Intermediate School, Berkeley

Janet Obata Teel
Albany Middle School, Albany

Camilla Thayer
Piedmont Middle School, Piedmont

Larry Zedaker
Piedmont Middle School, Piedmont

* Trial test coordinators

The following individuals also made important contributions to the development of these units, as part a mid-career teaching credential program at Mills College (see Acknowledgments for further details).

Mills College Department of Education
Jane Bowyer
Betty Karplus
Claire Smith

Class Members:

1988–89

John Cypher, Marianne Gielow, Margaret Hellweg, Dick Holmquist, Yvette McCullough, Annie Peterson, Simone Saunders, Alfreda Stephens-Surge, Robert Stewart, Jennifer Wilson

1989–90

Lynn Allan, Lisa Aronow, Richard Bell, Bob Brewer, Lejla Cyr, Steven Eiger, Vincent Haskell, Peter Hollingsworth, Jefferey Knoth, Dennis Kohlmann, Karen Kyker, Sandi Metaxas, Eleanor Rasmussen, Wendy Struhl, Timothy Tisher, Jeff Winemiller

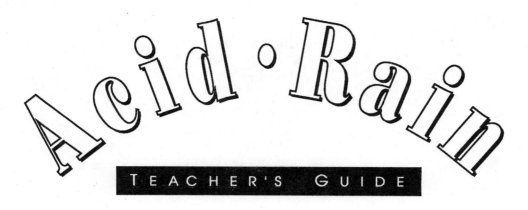

Acid · Rain

TEACHER'S GUIDE

Grades 6–10

Skills
Observing, Measuring and Recording Data, Experimenting, Classifying, Drawing Conclusions, Synthesizing Information, Role-Playing, Problem Solving, Critical Thinking, Decision-Making, Brainstorming Solutions

Concepts
Acid, Base, Neutral, pH, Neutralize, Buffering Capacity, Ecosystem, Effect of Acid Rain on Plants, Animals, and Lakes, Environmental Issues

Themes
Systems and Interactions, Models and Simulations, Patterns of Change, Stability, Diversity and Unity, Matter, Energy, Evolution, Scale

Nature of Science and Mathematics
Scientific Community, Science and Technology, Changing Nature of Facts and Theories, Creativity and Constraints, Theory-Based and Testable, Cooperative Efforts, Objectivity and Ethics, Real-Life Applications, Interdisciplinary

WHAT ARE THEMES?
Themes can be seen as major, recurring ideas that provide a framework for the science curriculum. For more on what GEMS means by themes, please see page... **147**

Time
Eight 50-minute sessions

Colin Hocking
Jacqueline Barber
Jan Coonrod

LHS GEMS

Great Explorations in Math and Science (GEMS)
Lawrence Hall of Science
University of California at Berkeley

Illustrations
Carol Bevilacqua
Rose Craig

Photographs
Richard Hoyt
Colin Hocking
Lincoln Bergman
Grace Alba

Lawrence Hall of Science, University of California, Berkeley, CA 94720. Chairman: Glenn T. Seaborg; Director: Marian C. Diamond

Initial support for the origination and publication of the GEMS series was provided by the A.W. Mellon Foundation and the Carnegie Corporation of New York. GEMS has also received support from the McDonnell Douglas Foundation and the McDonnell Douglas Employees Community Fund, the Hewlett Packard Company Foundation, and the people at Chevron USA. GEMS also gratefully acknowledges the contribution of word processing equipment from Apple Computer, Inc. This support does not imply responsibility for statements or views expressed in publications of the GEMS program. Under a grant from the National Science Foundation, GEMS Leader's Workshops have been held across the country. For further information on GEMS leadership opportunities, or to receive a publication brochure and the *GEMS Network News*, please contact GEMS at the address and phone number below.

International Standard Book Number: 0-912511-74-5

COMMENTS WELCOME

Great Explorations in Math and Science (GEMS) is an ongoing curriculum development project. GEMS guides are revised periodically, to incorporate teacher comments and new approaches. We welcome your criticisms, suggestions, helpful hints, and any anecdotes about your experience presenting GEMS activities. Your suggestions will be reviewed each time a GEMS guide is revised. Please send your comments to: GEMS Revisions, c/o Lawrence Hall of Science, University of California, Berkeley, CA 94720. The phone number is (510) 642-7771.

Great Explorations in Math and Science (GEMS) Program

The Lawrence Hall of Science (LHS) is a public science center on the University of California at Berkeley campus. LHS offers a full program of activities for the public, including workshops and classes, exhibits, films, lectures, and special events. LHS is also a center for teacher education and curriculum research and development.

Over the years, LHS staff have developed a multitude of activities, assembly programs, classes, and interactive exhibits. These programs have proven to be successful at the Hall and should be useful to schools, other science centers, museums, and community groups. A number of these guided-discovery activities have been published under the Great Explorations in Math and Science (GEMS) title, after an extensive refinement process that includes classroom testing of trial versions, modifications to ensure the use of easy-to-obtain materials, and carefully written and edited step-by-step instructions and background information to allow presentation by teachers without special background in mathematics or science.

Staff
Glenn T. Seaborg, **Principal Investigator**
Jacqueline Barber, **Director**
Cary Sneider, **Curriculum Specialist**
Katharine Barrett, John Erickson, Jaine Kopp, Kimi Hosoume, Laura Lowell, Linda Lipner, Laura Tucker, Carolyn Willard,
Staff Development Specialists
Jan M. Goodman, **Mathematics Consultant**
Cynthia Ashley, **Administrative Coordinator**
Gabriela Solomon, **Distribution Coordinator**
Lisa Haderlie Baker, **Art Director**
Carol Bevilacqua and Lisa Klofkorn, **Designers**
Lincoln Bergman and Kay Fairwell, **Editors**

Contributing Authors
Jacqueline Barber
Katharine Barrett
Lincoln Bergman
Jaine Kopp
Linda Lipner
Laura Lowell
Linda De Lucchi
Jean Echols
Jan M. Goodman
Alan Gould
Kimi Hosoume
Sue Jagoda
Larry Malone
Cary I. Sneider
Jennifer Meux White
Carolyn Willard

Acknowledgments

The original "Fake Lakes" activity that serves at the core of this unit was first developed in 1987 by one of the authors, Jan Coonrod. This activity was expanded to create a longer unit of study by Jan Coonrod, Evelyn Kavaler, Jacqueline Barber and other Lawrence Hall of Science staff as part of an NSF-funded project conducted jointly with Mills College in Oakland, California (grant # TEI 875 1487). Through this project, entitled "The Mid-Career Mathematics and Science Program," a number of units were developed and presented as part of a teaching credential program, designed to model the integrated teaching of mathematics and various fields of science. Mills College staff of this project and the mid-career professionals enrolled in this pre-service program also gave valuable feedback on the activities. These individuals are listed in the front of the guide following the listing of teachers who tested this unit in their classrooms.

The unit as it appears in this guide was further evolved by Jacqueline Barber, Colin Hocking, and other members of the GEMS staff. Colin Hocking worked on this unit while on leave from the Centre for Communications and Applied Science, Holmesglen College of Technical and Further Education, Melbourne, Australia. Grace Alba spent time refining the equipment used in the Fake Lakes activity, working out details of seed germination, and researching suggestions for soil collection in different regions around the nation. She and Kevin Beals both worked on making the background information in the "Behind the Scenes" section readable, and Kevin Beals also lent his talents to enlivening the lake animals play. Carolyn Willard also provided important input to the refinement of these activities. The development of the play and its use to encourage discussion were inspired by activities in "Social Implications of Technology," published in 1987 by the Ministry of Education, Victoria, Australia. The "Startling Statements" game, presented in Session 3, is modeled after activities developed by the EQUALS staff of the Lawrence Hall of Science. The limericks about acid rain that appear on the back cover were written by the GEMS Principal Editor, Lincoln Bergman.

Special thanks to Meg Andersen of East Falmouth, Massachusetts, who wrote us to correct a small inaccuracy that appeared in the background section of the first edition. In this second edition, we have also added a section on possible "Literature Connections," beginning on page 144.

Contents

Introduction

Acid rain is much more than a topic of study. It's a serious environmental problem that affects the quality of our lives and the health of the ecosystems on which we and future generations depend. Our young people need to know about acid rain, because they will become the policy-makers and voting citizens of the future. And investigating acid rain provides an excellent forum for learning important and useful concepts in chemistry, ecology, biology, mathematics, and even social studies.

In one sense, the problem of acid rain is straightforward—certain airborne pollutants produced by cars, power plants, and industry react with sunlight and moisture to form acid. This acid mixes with and dissolves in the water of rain, snow, hail, sleet, and fog and falls to the earth. But when we begin to ask questions, the complexity of the problem of acid rain becomes more evident. How *acid* is acid rain? What are the factors that influence the acidity of rain? Does the pollution from cars produce the same kind of acid rain as the pollution from coal-burning power plants? Where I live there's no polluting industry—does that mean there is no acid rain? What are the effects of acid rain on animals? plants? humans? ecosystems?

Engaged and Empowered

Perhaps the biggest challenge in presenting any environmental problem to students is to do so in a way that encourages them to feel engaged and empowered, rather than discouraged or overwhelmed. In this context, acid rain is a good problem for students to tackle. Although it is a very serious problem that has already caused severe damage, significant improvements have been made in air quality in recent years, while research continues and preliminary efforts are underway to investigate other solutions. The future need not be viewed as bleak. Acid rain is also a problem that each one of us can have a personal role in addressing, by finding ways to conserve energy. In this unit, your students, who are growing up in a time of increasing concern about the environment, combine the personal and the social by working together to explore possible solutions and practice making decisions.

In designing this unit, we placed emphasis on having students brainstorm solutions, tapping into the considerable creative energies of young people. We've also included a variety of activity formats (lab experiments, discussions, writing, role-playing, a game, and reading a play) that, our experience and testing tells us, will keep group pacing and spirits up. Many teachers and educational researchers have found that presenting a variety of learning formats, connected to everyday social concerns, is also an excellent way to value and bridge the varying backgrounds and experiences of boys and girls, and minority groups, in the classroom.

Finally, the total experience of the unit is a very enabling one. Students engage in activities that lead them to discover the problem of acid rain for themselves, to generate possible solutions, to critically evaluate those solutions, and then to formulate their own opinions about what should be done. The problem-solving, critical thinking, and decision-making skills that are developed and practiced in this unit are skills that empower students in many parts of their lives.

Session by Session: Unit Overview

Students begin the unit by writing down everything they have heard about acid rain, and questions they have about it. These lists are added to, and modified, throughout the unit, as knowledge changes and as new questions arise. In the last session, students examine these lists to see how their understandings have changed, and discuss further questions and areas of investigation. Starting the unit with this listing allows you to begin with your students' current knowledge and misconceptions and build from there. It also communicates to students that in science, framing good questions can be as important a task as finding good answers.

Also in the first session, students set up an experiment in which they observe the effect of a common acid (vinegar) of various concentrations on seed germination. The seed experiment continues throughout much of the unit, giving students something to watch and reflect on each day.

Homework assigned at the end of Session 1 involves students in searching their homes for things they can identify as acids. In Session 2, the students learn more about what acids are, and how to measure their strength, by conducting tests on common substances using Universal Indicator solution. The class adds their data to a large, butcher paper pH chart, which is used as a reference throughout the unit. After this session, students have a working knowledge of the pH scale, the pH of common acids, and of the concept of neutralizing acids.

In Session 3, students play a game called, "Startling Statements." In this game, each student wears a question on her back, and collects responses to that question from other students in the class. By speculating on the answers to these questions first, students become eager to know what the answers might be. The class then compares their own views to those of the scientific community. This game provides an engaging and active way of delivering information about acid rain to students. Students go on to read an article about acid rain, as homework following this session.

Session 4 involves students in experimenting with model lakes, or what are referred to as "fake" lakes. They investigate what effects different soil types have on the pH of lakes and discover that some soils are naturally acidic while others contain natural buffers (acid-neutralizing substances). Then, they see what happens to lake pH after an acid rainstorm. By modeling a lake system (lake water, surrounding soil, and rain water), and experimenting with its different components, students learn that the pH of rainwater is not the only factor that determines whether or not a lake or a region is at risk of damage. At the end of the session, students add a buffer tablet (Tums®—which is mostly calcium carbonate) to some of the lakes, replicating a common treatment for acidic lakes in Europe and the United States. At the beginning of the next session, they observe the effect the buffer had on acidity in each lake.

Students also spend time in Session 5 collecting results and drawing conclusions from the seed germination experiment begun in Session 1. The class goes on to begin preparing for an emergency town meeting to be held in Session 7, called to address the problem of acid rain. The scene is set in Session 5 when you read a description of Laketown, where the meeting will take place. Situated near the mountains, Laketown has an active fishing and tourist industry, and a developing heavy industry, including one manufacturer of records, CD disks, and recording tapes. The students choose which interest group they'd like to represent: the manufacturers, the fishing people, the politicians, or the townspeople. They are given a set of instructions for how to prepare for the coming town meeting, and some time to begin. For homework, the students read an article about solutions to the problem of acid rain, and jot down a list of solutions they will propose to their interest group.

Session 6 begins with a class brainstorm of possible solutions to the problem of acid rain. This is followed by a dramatic reading of a play about acid rain that takes place in an imaginary setting. Plants and animals, living in and near a lake threatened by acid rain, meet to discuss their future. By introducing information about the effect of acidity on aquatic plants and animals, the play enriches students' understanding of the physical modeling of lake systems provided by the fake lakes experiment. The play also exemplifies stereotypical human responses to environmental issues, as represented by the roles played by the various lake characters, which provides the basis for discussing the constructive and non-constructive roles played by members of a community. This leads smoothly into a town meeting planning session in which the four interest groups meet again to prepare for the town meeting.

The town meeting takes place in Session 7. As mayor of the town, you facilitate a structured interchange between interest groups in which each group has an opportunity to present its point of view, propose one or more solutions, and ask questions of other interest groups. The focus here is on finding commonly acceptable solutions and outlining the areas of conflict and disagreement, rather than competing for audience approval or winning debating points.

In Session 8, students put aside their town meeting roles, and participate in a straw poll to determine which possible solutions they **personally** think are best. Their recent experiences of step-by-step planning to discuss the complexities of the issues, and the town meeting itself, help prepare students to critically discuss solutions to the problem of acid rain **from their own viewpoints.** Then, together as a class, they review the ongoing lists of questions and statements about acid rain, and go on to generate ideas for imagined scientific experiments or technologies that could help solve problems posed by acid rain.

Timing and Preparation

As you proceed through the unit, you will want to adjust the activities and their time frame to the needs of your particular group of students. While we found that eight 50-minute sessions were adequate for many of our trial groups, it was not for all. The interests and capabilities of sixth graders who conducted these activities were very different from those of tenth graders. They were slower at some activities and took less time with others. For some groups, at various points, the discussions flowed quite well; in others, students did not have much to say. Students who were less accustomed to experimental activities often took longer to complete them and occasionally became so excited that it was difficult for the teachers to have them discuss their results in the same session. Be aware that you might find yourself short of time in some sessions, and may need to schedule an additional session or partial session to present the information and issues adequately. On the other hand, you may find that your students go through the activities faster than you expect. You will know how best to adjust the timing for your group of students.

Similarly, we found in testing this unit that students who were used to working in small groups had no trouble preparing and conducting the town meeting, while students without much practice in group work needed more structure and assistance from the teacher. You may also need to adjust this part of the unit for your particular group of students.

Where to Begin

Before starting *Acid Rain* with your students, we suggest that you: 1) read through the entire teacher's guide including the background information about acid rain in the section entitled, "Behind the Scenes," 2) gather the equipment and materials you will need, enlisting student help where possible, and 3) try out the lab activities in Session 2 and Session 4 yourself. There are several items that may need to be ordered (Universal Indicator solution and a solution of sulfuric acid) and some items that may need to be "scrounged" (a class set of white styrofoam egg cartons or other reaction trays, and sentence strips). You will also need to collect several different soil samples, or have your students assist you in this task. You will want to have these materials in hand before you begin. The rest of the materials used in the unit are commonly available, including things like coffee filters, vinegar, and seeds. Also, be advised that the sessions involving hands-on science experiments take a fair amount of preparation. While the single-subject science teachers who trial tested the unit did not feel this amount of preparation was excessive, many of the multiple-subject trial teachers found that it required significantly more time than they expected. See the "Important Note About Preparation" on page 6 for ideas that might help you reduce the time required for preparation.

Another GEMS unit, *Of Cabbages and Chemistry,* provides a series of activities that can be used to introduce students to the concepts of acids, bases, and neutrals in a guided discovery fashion. Some teachers have found it useful to present the activities in *Of Cabbages and Chemistry* to their students **before** beginning the *Acid Rain* unit. If you do this, you will need to adjust some of the activities and discussions in this unit. Several suggestions about how to modify activities for students who are knowledgeable about acidity and pH are provided in the guide.

No Special Background Needed!

You do not need to have a background in chemistry, ecology, or anything scientific to present this unit to your students! The background material contained in the "Behind the Scenes" section on page 123 provides all the information you need to feel comfortable in presenting this unit to your students. Keep in mind that the background section is intended to provide you with a base of information. Because acid rain is a topic about which much is still unknown, and research is ongoing, this section will not necessarily have the most current information available. That's okay for the purposes of presenting a unit to 6th—10th graders. If you would like to be more up-to-date, find one or two recent articles on acid rain to catch up on the latest information. Not only is it okay for you **not** to be an expert on the topic of acid rain, there is great value in your learning along with your students and modeling for them that no one knows all the answers—learning is a lifelong experience.

Many excellent activity tangents and extensions are suggested in "Going Further," on page 120. You may want to look these over at the start if your students have already studied acids, bases, pH, and/or acid rain.

"Summary Outlines" are provided to help you guide your students through these activities in an organized way. Student data sheets are provided immediately following the session in which they are needed.

Whether you are presenting this unit as part of a general science program, a chemistry course, a life science course, or a social studies class, we hope you will enjoy the integrated nature of the material and the excitement of learning science, mathematics, social issues, and the important lifelong skills of critical thinking, problem-solving, and decision-making through exploration of a real and pressing environmental issue.

Or to put it more lightly, in limerick:

There once was an oxide called SOx
Who, along with another named NOx,
Unleashed acid rain,
As this guide will explain,
Causing "eco-illogical" shocks.

From smokestacks and auto exhaust
Exacting a terrible cost
Acid rain's killing lakes
Do we have what it takes—
To make certain that no more get lost?

The tough problems posed by pollution
Are crying out loud for solution
To bring NOx and SOx down
Let us meet in our town
For we each have a key contribution.

Time Frame

Please see the note about variable time frames in the "Introduction" to this guide. Other suggestions appear in overviews to each session.

Session 1: Pick Your Brain About Acid Rain

Teacher Preparation	30 minutes
Class Activity	50 minutes
Homework Assignment	30 minutes

Session 2: Introduction to Acidity and pH

Teacher Preparation	45 minutes (first time taught)
	25 minutes (subsequent times)
Class Activity	50 minutes

Session 3: Startling Statements About Acid Rain

Teacher Preparation	40 minutes (first time taught)
	5 minutes (subsequent times)
Class Activity	50 minutes
Homework Assignment	15 minutes

Session 4: Fake Lakes

Teacher Preparation	60 minutes (first time taught)
	30 minutes (subsequent times)
Class Activity	50 minutes

Session 5: Welcome to Laketown!

Teacher Preparation	10 minutes
Class Activity	50 minutes
Homework Assignment	20 minutes

Session 6: The Salamanders Have Their Say

Teacher Preparation	10 minutes
Class Activity	50 minutes

Session 7: Town Meeting: Making Community Decisions

Teacher Preparation	10 minutes
Class Activity	50 minutes

Session 8: "Everything You've Always Wanted to Know About Acid Rain . . ."

Teacher Preparation	10 minutes
Class Activity	50 minutes

An Important Note about Preparation

The first time you teach this unit, you are likely to find that the amount of preparation required is considerable. You might find one or more of the following time-saving suggestions helpful:

- Coordinate the presentation of the unit with another teacher at your school and share the preparation tasks (and/or teach it to several classes concurrently, if possible).

- Start acquiring and preparing materials early, so you can accomplish the tasks at a more gradual pace.

- Have several of your students help you prepare materials in the days or weeks preceding the unit. You may want to give students extra credit for helping with these tasks.

- If you have access to a photocopying machine, duplicate labels onto blank sheets of self-adhesive mailing labels, using the master label sheets located at the back of this guide.

- Rinse the labeled cups and bottles after they are used and carefully reorganize the "Startling Statements" signs. Save them to use next time you present the unit.

- Offer to lend the materials to another teacher in your school who might be interested in presenting this unit.

The time needed for preparation will be greatly reduced in subsequent presentations, as much of it involves one-time tasks. As with other hands-on science activities, the effort you put into planning and presenting *Acid Rain* will be amply rewarded by the increase in your students' enthusiasm for, and understanding of, science.

Please note: A few of the photographs used in this guide show students using equipment that has since been modified or simplified. These students took part in earlier trial versions of these activities. Accurate equipment descriptions and specifications are found in the "What You Need" sections of each session, which in most cases include accompanying drawings.

Session 1: Pick Your Brain About Acid Rain

Overview

In this session, students are encouraged to recall anything they have heard about acid rain, and to come up with questions about it. Not only is this the usual starting place for investigations in science, it also provides teachers with a way to find out what students already know, and what misconceptions they may have. In small groups, students discover what their classmates have also heard and begin to explore and synthesize some initial information about acid rain.

From group reports, the teacher compiles a class list of statements and questions about acid rain. This list serves as a useful tool for students to sort out the scientific validity of hearsay information, and, as the unit progresses, to correct misconceptions and separate factual information from statements more related to social values.

In the last 15 minutes of the session, students set up a plant growth experiment. The goal of the experiment is to investigate the effects of various dilutions of vinegar on seed germination. Students monitor the experiment throughout the first half of the unit, and in Session 5 they summarize results and draw conclusions. A homework assignment to introduce the subject of acids and prepare students for Session 2 is passed out at the end of the session.

A word about the sequence and timing of the session. The first part of the activity, in which your students come up with and discuss statements and questions about acid rain, may take more or less time, depending on what your students have to say. If this takes more time than we've projected, it may result in a fairly crowded session. **You will need about 15 minutes at the end to set up the plant growth experiment.** Because we are aware that many teachers will want their students to do more than hold discussions in this first session, we suggest you stop wherever you are 15 minutes before the end, and begin the plant growth experiment. Further discussion of student statements and questions can happen later in the day or at the beginning of the next session. On the other hand, if your students are involved in an intense discussion, you could also postpone the plant growth experiment.

The purposes of Session 1 are to: (1) begin the investigations in this unit with your students' initial understandings and questions; (2) provide a basis for students to sort through the complex, science-related social issues of acid rain, distinguishing between incorrect, factual, and value statements; (3) encourage discussion and make use of a variety of learning modes in investigating the range of scientific issues brought into focus by the topic of acid rain; and (4) involve students in experimenting with real materials so they can observe firsthand some effects of acid on plant growth.

What You Need

For the class:

- [ ] 30 or 40 sheets of blank paper (at least one for each student, with several to spare)
- [ ] 1 graduated cylinder
- [ ] 5 empty, clean 8–10 oz glass bottles (such as those used to contain mineral water)
- [ ] four or five large sheets of butcher paper
- [ ] a marking pen
- [ ] masking tape
- [ ] scissors
- [ ] about 150 milliliters of white distilled vinegar
- [ ] about 300 milliliters of tap water
- [ ] access to a sink or 1 cottage cheese or other small wide-mouthed container for collecting waste solutions

For each group of 4 students:

- [ ] 1 cafeteria tray
- [ ] 2 clear plastic wide-mouthed cups (about 9 oz. capacity)
- [ ] 1 marking pen that can write on plastic cups
- [ ] 2 pieces of paper towel, large enough to fit into the bottom of the plastic cups
- [ ] 2 sheets of plastic wrap, large enough to easily cover the tops of the plastic cups
- [ ] 20 seeds (provide half the groups with sunflower seeds and the other half with pea seeds). Use seeds from packets of gardening seeds. Don't use dried seeds intended for eating, unless you find beforehand by testing them that they have high germination rates.
- [ ] 5 or more "sentence strips" (Sentence strips are commercially available. They are strips of light card stock approximately 24" long and 3" wide. See the "Resources" section on page 142 for ordering information. Or, you can make your own by cutting strips of butcher paper or newsprint. The exact size is unimportant.)

For each student:

- [ ] 1 "Acids in Your Life" homework sheet (master provided, page 19)

Getting Ready

Several Weeks Before the Activity

You may want to help increase the interest and motivation of your students by announcing that a unit on acid rain will start in several weeks. Suggest that they bring in magazine or newspaper articles on acid rain, for posting in class. You could display a large, blank sheet of butcher paper on one wall with the heading, "COMING SOON—ACID RAIN!" and put up on the sheet any articles you and your students find. CAUTION: **Do not make this activity into a formal assignment,** or you will sabotage the effectiveness of the first session. This session will not work as planned if it takes place after assigned readings, as students will tend to focus on what they are "supposed" to know, rather than experiencing a more open session for thinking and wondering about what they've heard.

Before the Day of the Activity

1. Cut the paper towels into squares, so each square fits easily into the bottom of a plastic cup. While the corners of the toweling can come up on the sides of the cup, the piece of towel should fit more or less flatly, covering the bottom of the cup.

2. Cut the plastic wrap into squares, so each piece easily fits over the top of a plastic cup, and down the sides. The plastic wrap does not have to make an airtight seal over the cup, but it does need to have sufficient overlap to remain in place.

3. Find a clear, warm area, outside of direct sunlight and safe from disturbance, to put the plant growth experiment until it is examined in Session 5. Preferably, select an area accessible to the students, so they can monitor results as the unit progresses.

4. If your class meets in the same room for each session of this unit, try to find a space on one wall where you can post the student statements and questions arising from this session, so the lists can be referred to in future sessions. If this is not possible, at least make sure that they are recorded on paper (as described below), and stored safely so they can be posted during later sessions in the unit.

5. Label the five small bottles as follows: "100% vinegar," "20% vinegar," "5% vinegar," "1% vinegar," and "water."

6. Fill each of the five vinegar and water bottles with 100 mls of the appropriate contents:

- 100% vinegar— 100 ml vinegar
- 20% vinegar— 20 ml vinegar/80 ml tap water
- 5% vinegar— 5 ml vinegar/95 ml tap water
- 1% vinegar— 1 ml vinegar/99 ml tap water
- water— 100 ml tap water

Cover the mouth of each bottle with plastic wrap.

7. Duplicate enough copies of the "Acids in Your Life" homework sheet (master included, page 19) so there is one for every student in your class.

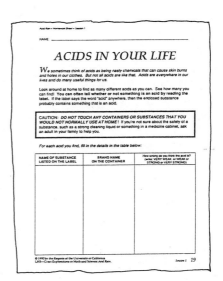

On the Day of the Activity

1. Set out one tray for each group of four students. On each tray, place two plastic cups, two pieces of paper towel, and two pieces of plastic wrap. Set these trays aside for later.

2. In a centrally-located place in the room, preferably near a sink, set up an area where students can pour the vinegar and water solutions from the bottles containing the solutions. Set the bottle of vinegar here as well. If you don't have a sink in your room, provide a cottage-cheese or other wide-mouthed container into which waste solution can be poured.

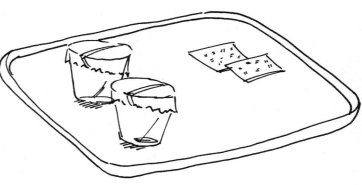

3. Put the sunflower and pea seeds in an area where students from every group can come and count them out.

You or a student could also transcribe the listing of student statements and questions about acid rain onto overhead transparencies or a smaller sheet of paper that could be duplicated.

4. Post several sheets of butcher paper on the wall. Set a marking pen nearby for recording students' ideas and questions. Also place the sentence strips, the rest of the marking pens, and masking tape here for later use.

5. Arrange the room by pushing desks together or moving tables so there is one flat work area for each group of four students.

Pick Your Brain

Introduce the Challenge of the Day

1. Introduce the topic by telling the class that you want to find out what they've heard about *acid rain*. Emphasize that this is the same way that scientists start an investigation, by finding out what they already know, in order to figure out what to investigate next, and how to do it.

2. Stress that you are asking for what they've **heard** about acid rain, not necessarily what they know for sure. Anything that they've heard about the topic from books, TV, newspapers, or word of mouth is acceptable.

3. Explain that each student is to write down what they've heard about acid rain. It doesn't have to be long or complicated. They have about three minutes to make a list of everything that comes to mind. No one else will read their list; it's to help collect their thoughts for the next part of the activity (so tell them not to worry about using whole sentences).

Note: Some students may need additional reassurance that it is okay to write down things that may not turn out to be accurate. Remind them that the purpose of the unit is to find out what is and is not accurate in reports and conversations about acid rain, and one good starting point is what the students remember having heard about it.

4. Ask the students if they have any questions about what they are supposed to do. Distribute pieces of blank paper and have them begin.

5. If some students have run out of things to write (or they don't have any statements to write in the first place) tell them to turn over the paper and write down **questions** they have about acid rain.

Organize a "Mind Swap"

1. After three minutes (or up to five or six minutes if many students are still writing, or shorter if many students are finished sooner) have the students put their pencils down.

2. Explain that they are going to be working in teams, to combine what they have heard, and to find out from each other if anyone knows the answers to any of their questions. Tell them that, in groups of three or four, they will do something called a "mind swap."

3. Explain the rules as follows: In each group, one student begins by sharing all she has heard about acid rain. No one is to interrupt the speaker or discuss anything yet. The other members of the group listen and, if they wish, can add things the speaker has on her list, to their own lists. After one person finishes sharing, the next person has a turn, until all in the group share what was on their lists. After all group members have shared, they can then ask each other questions and discuss some of what they each had to say.

4. If your class is not already organized into teams of three to four students each, help them do that now.

5. Make it clear that this is a team activity, not a full class discussion. Ask if there are any questions about what the groups will be doing, then have the groups begin.

In quite a few of the classes whose teachers helped test this unit, students came up with the statement, "acid rain makes your hair turn green." Reportedly, there was an incident in one of the most popular network television situation comedies in which a character shampoos her hair using rain water that she had placed in a copper bowl. The rain turns out to be acid rain and because it corrodes the copper bowl, a greenish color results. Thus, the misconception that it was the acid rain itself that turned the hair green. The fact that this statement was cited so widely, in different schools and grade levels, is an indication of the immense power of television to influence ideas, unfortunately not always in the most accurate or constructive ways. Given the ubiquitous reruns of top shows, we wouldn't be surprised if your students now and in the future continue to have "heard" that acid rain has this rather startling effect.

The TV story line does suggest an additional activity you could carry out regarding the effects of acid on metals. Place pennies in separate plastic cups, and pour various dilutions of vinegar in the cups, to just cover the penny. Observe over time to see the effects of the acid on the metal in the pennies. See "Going Further" on page 120 for a related suggestion.

Share What Everyone Has "Heard"

1. After about five minutes, stop the group activity. Calling on each group in turn, ask a student to say one thing that their group has heard about acid rain.

2. List these on a large sheet of paper, to keep for reference as the unit develops. Continue asking each group in turn for a statement, until everything has been recorded on the paper. Tell the groups that it is okay to "pass," if all of their statements have already been said by someone else.

Note: You may want to have one or more students help you write up the statements on the paper, or have several students take over this task entirely, with your guidance.

3. Ask the students if they can see any two statements on the paper that can't both be true. Encourage discussion. Point out that there is often controversy and disagreement in science. You may also want to mention that sometimes we *think* we know something, and it *might* have been true at one time, but as knowledge in the scientific community grows, it is shown to be inaccurate. It is also very easy for people to confuse what they might know about acid rain with information about other environmental topics.

4. Point out that what the people in each group have been sharing is what they have *heard* to be true. Explain that, as the class continues its study of acid rain, they will be better able to determine whether or not any of the statements is correct.

Generate Questions: What We *Don't* Know About Acid Rain

1. Tell the class that you'd like them to work together to come up with questions about acid rain. While some of them may already have begun this individually, you'd like them to focus on it as a team.

2. Explain that the "rule" here is that a question can only be considered a question if no one in the group has an acceptable answer. So, each group will need to discuss each question to see if anyone might know the answer. Ask each group to come up with at least one question per person.

3. Ask each group to write their questions in large print on a sentence strip. Tell the class that, after about five minutes, you will ask each group to post their written questions on a large sheet of paper on the wall.

4. Check for any questions about what the students will be doing. Distribute the markers and strips of paper, and have them begin.

Post the Questions

1. After about five minutes of group discussion, regain the attention of the class and have the groups post their questions. If you have time, you may want to sort these questions into groups or categories, such as technical questions about acid rain, questions about its effects, questions about the future, questions about possible solutions to the acid rain problem, etc.

2. If you do not have time to deal with the questions further in this session, ask the students to post them, and come back to them as part of your introduction to Session 2. Make sure that you have sufficient time before the end of Session 1 (about 15 minutes) for the class to set up the plant growth experiment. However you decide to proceed, make sure you save all of the student statements and questions recorded in this session, so you can refer back to them in later sessions. If possible, find a permanent place to post them on the classroom wall, until the unit is completed. If not, be sure they are recorded on butcher paper so you can post them at appropriate times.

3. After all groups have posted their questions, ask if anyone in the class can offer a response to any of them. Tell the class that you will return to this list several times during the unit, to see which questions the group thinks they can then answer.

4. Point out that scientists and others working on the acid rain problem also have many questions, and do not know all of the answers—that's one of the reasons why acid rain is a difficult problem.

Here is an example of a list of student statements and questions about acid rain, generated by a 7th grade class.

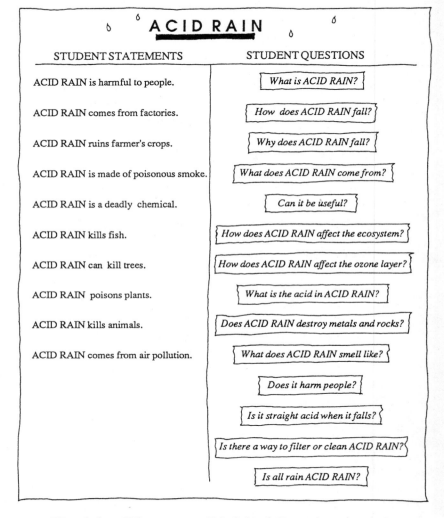

Healthy Plants or Pickled Beansprouts?

Introduce the Plant Growth Experiment

1. Have the students remain in their original teams. Tell them they are about to begin their first experimental investigation of acid rain. They will investigate the effects of various strengths of acid on the first stages of growth (or germination) of some seeds, to find out firsthand whether or not the acid affects growth.

2. Show the students a bottle of vinegar, and point out that vinegar is an acid, called acetic acid. Explain that today the class will begin germinating seeds in various solutions of vinegar and water, to see how this affects their growth. Mention that later in the unit they will compare the strength of the acid in vinegar with the strength of acid in acid rain.

Explain the Experimental Procedure

1. Explain to the class how to set up a "germination trial" in the groups. Each group is to set up two trials: one, a control trial using tap water, and the other using a particular dilution of vinegar (from 100% vinegar to 1% vinegar). You may want to explain how you made the vinegar dilutions. (If your students are not familiar with percentages, use fractions or other words to describe the dilutions.)

2. Show the groups how to label their two cups with the name of the test solution that will be added, the type of seed to be tested, and some identifying symbol for their group.

3. Explain that each group will take two plastic cups, fit each with one layer of paper towel, and add test solution (either tap water or some pre-determined strength of vinegar solution) until there is about one quarter of an inch of the liquid in the bottom of the cup (equivalent to about 10 ml, depending on the size of cup you use). While this need not be exact, ask students to pour carefully and double check to see there is about a quarter-inch of liquid covering the toweling. (You might want to point out that a quarter-inch is about half the width of your thumbnail.) Then the students will count out and add ten undamaged seeds (with coats intact) to each cup. Finally, each cup will be covered with plastic wrap, to reduce evaporation (*Note:* It is not necessary for the wrap to be airtight.)

4. Each group will need to designate one person to obtain the test solutions, one person to label the cups, one person to obtain and count out the seeds, and one person to prepare and fit the paper towel into the cup and stretch the plastic wrap over the cup after the solution and seeds are inside.

It is has been our experience that most sunflower seeds float in water. This is not a problem, as their buoyancy does not seem to affect their germination.

If you have extra time at the end of the session, you may want to ask the class to write an hypothesis, predicting what they think will happen for each of the combinations of solutions and seed types in the experiment. These predictions can be compared with the actual results when the seeds are examined in Session 5, and could form a basis for discussing the effects of acid rain on living organisms.

5. Tell each group which type of seed they will use and which vinegar solution (at least two groups should have 100% vinegar).

6. Ask the class to summarize the procedure. Distribute the equipment to each group, and have them begin.

Groups Set Up the Germination Trials

1. As the groups set up the experiment, check to see that each cup is correctly labelled on the outside with the solution that was added to it. Also check to make sure that students pour in the right amount of solution so there is about one-quarter inch of liquid above the paper towelling.

2. When the students finish, have them put their seed trial cups in a warm place where the cups will not be disturbed, but will be accessible so students can observe what happens to the seeds over the course of the unit.

Introduce the Homework Assignment

1. Point out to the students that in order to gain a better understanding of acid rain, it's first necessary to learn more about what an acid is. That will be the focus of the next session.

2. In preparation for this, there is some homework. Show them the "Acids in Your Life" homework sheet, and explain that you'd like them to look around in their homes, or in a grocery store or supermarket, for things that they think are acids, and record them on the sheet. You may want to emphasize portions of the instructions that are on the homework sheet, particularly regarding safety, by reading them out loud to the class.

3. Distribute the homework sheets and ask the students to complete them by the next class session.

NAME: _____

ACIDS IN YOUR LIFE

W*e sometimes think of acids as being nasty chemicals that can cause skin burns and holes in our clothes. But not all acids are like that. Acids are everywhere in our lives and do many useful things for us.*

Look around at home to find as many different acids as you can. See how many you can find! **You can often tell whether or not something is an acid by reading the label.** If the label says the word "acid" anywhere, then the enclosed substance probably contains something that is an acid.

CAUTION: ***DO NOT TOUCH ANY CONTAINERS OR SUBSTANCES THAT YOU WOULD NOT NORMALLY USE AT HOME*** ! If you're not sure about the safety of a substance, such as a strong cleaning liquid or something in a medicine cabinet, ask an adult in your family to help you.

For each acid you find, fill in the details in the table below:

NAME OF SUBSTANCE LISTED ON THE LABEL	BRAND NAME ON THE CONTAINER	How strong do you think the acid is? (write: VERY WEAK or WEAK or STRONG or VERY STRONG)

Session 2: Introduction to Acidity and pH

Overview

In this session, students use Universal Indicator solution to measure the pH of various everyday solutions, including vinegar, lemon juice, baking soda solution, tap water, and normal rain water. Their findings, and the pH values of other substances, are posted on a large butcher paper pH chart. Students gain a working knowledge of pH, and a better understanding of what acids and bases are and how their strength can be measured.

By observing a simple demonstration, students learn why *normal rain* water is slightly acidic, and that this slight acidity can be beneficial. The range of pH values of *acid rain* is also posted on the chart.

If there is time, you may want to introduce the concepts of neutralization and buffers. However, if you feel this might be too much for your students to assimilate in one session, you can introduce these concepts later in the unit.

To build on student curiosity and interest, several "Going Further" activities are suggested for this session that provide some firsthand experience with neutralization and buffers.

The purposes of this session are to: (1) start from students' everyday knowledge and experience to learn about acids, bases, and neutrals; (2) provide practice and familiarity with the concept and measurement of pH, the use of Universal Indicator solution, and the Universal Indicator color chart; (3) provide the scientific background and terminology necessary for understanding the range of acidity of acid rain; and (4) introduce the concepts of neutralization and buffering.

If you feel that your students already have a practical understanding of how acids and bases are detected by indicators and placed on the pH scale, you may want to quickly review how the pH scale is constructed, and where some common acids and bases lie on it, and then move directly to some of the activities suggested in the "Going Further" section for this session, on page 36.

As regards the sequence of the session, some teachers, with a particularly active or restless class, have found it best to begin the session almost immediately with the experimental activity (after a very brief discussion of the pH scale). If you think this is the best approach for your class, look carefully at the suggested sequencing and reorganize it as you think best.

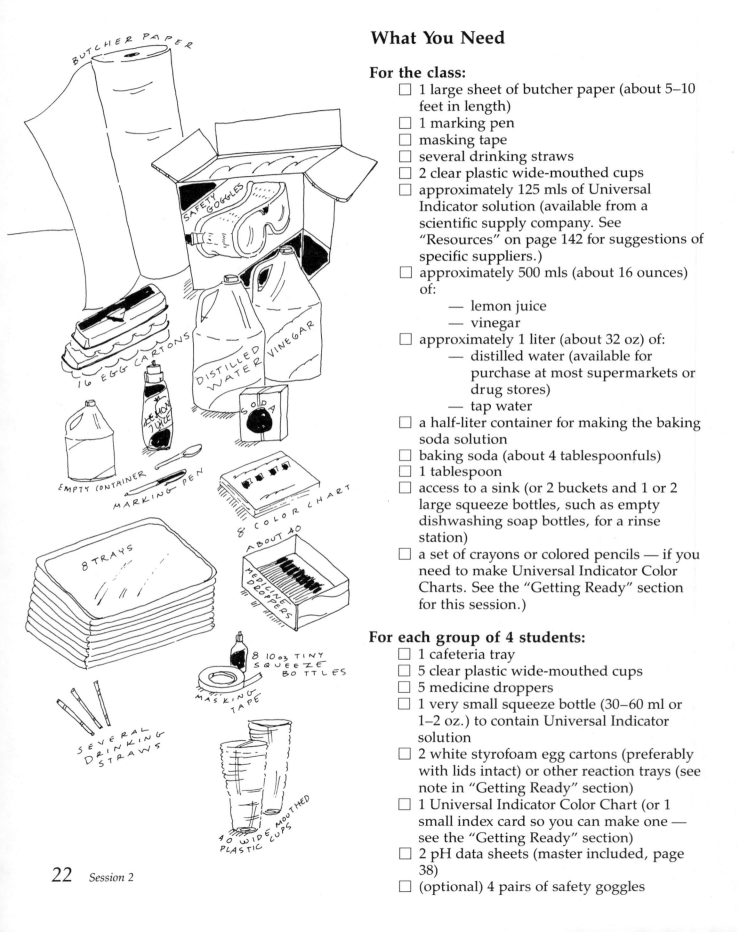

What You Need

For the class:

- ☐ 1 large sheet of butcher paper (about 5–10 feet in length)
- ☐ 1 marking pen
- ☐ masking tape
- ☐ several drinking straws
- ☐ 2 clear plastic wide-mouthed cups
- ☐ approximately 125 mls of Universal Indicator solution (available from a scientific supply company. See "Resources" on page 142 for suggestions of specific suppliers.)
- ☐ approximately 500 mls (about 16 ounces) of:
  - — lemon juice
  - — vinegar
- ☐ approximately 1 liter (about 32 oz) of:
  - — distilled water (available for purchase at most supermarkets or drug stores)
  - — tap water
- ☐ a half-liter container for making the baking soda solution
- ☐ baking soda (about 4 tablespoonfuls)
- ☐ 1 tablespoon
- ☐ access to a sink (or 2 buckets and 1 or 2 large squeeze bottles, such as empty dishwashing soap bottles, for a rinse station)
- ☐ a set of crayons or colored pencils — if you need to make Universal Indicator Color Charts. See the "Getting Ready" section for this session.)

For each group of 4 students:

- ☐ 1 cafeteria tray
- ☐ 5 clear plastic wide-mouthed cups
- ☐ 5 medicine droppers
- ☐ 1 very small squeeze bottle (30–60 ml or 1–2 oz.) to contain Universal Indicator solution
- ☐ 2 white styrofoam egg cartons (preferably with lids intact) or other reaction trays (see note in "Getting Ready" section)
- ☐ 1 Universal Indicator Color Chart (or 1 small index card so you can make one — see the "Getting Ready" section)
- ☐ 2 pH data sheets (master included, page 38)
- ☐ (optional) 4 pairs of safety goggles

Getting Ready

Several Weeks Before Beginning the Unit

Start collecting white styrofoam egg cartons for use as mixing trays. Try to keep the lids intact. Doing so gives you the option of asking the groups to close the covers when they have completed the activities, thus removing the temptation to "mix everything together to see what happens" while you are trying to focus their attention on a discussion of results. You can ask students to bring in cartons from home or contact restaurants that serve lots of breakfasts (fast food chain restaurants go through dozens of egg cartons per day). You can even contact egg farms. Other mixing trays can also be used, such as white plastic paint palettes, chemical reaction trays, or white ice cube trays.

Before the Day of the Activity

1. Make or Purchase Universal Indicator Color Charts. Sometimes Universal Indicator solution comes with color charts. If yours does not, or if you do not have a color chart for each team, then you will have to purchase or make some. To purchase color charts, consult the "Resources" section on page 142 for an inexpensive source of pH charts. To make color charts, consult the description on the side of the Universal Indicator container as to what color the indicator turns at each pH. Choose appropriately-colored crayons or pencils for each color, then make a color chart on index cards by aligning a swatch of these colors next to their pH reading (one chart for each group of four students). This task can be delegated to a student aide or to the students themselves, though it will definitely need to be done prior to this class session, as there is not enough time in the session for the students to do the class activities and complete this coloring task.

One enterprising teacher arranged to have rain samples sent to her from all over the country. Her students then tested the samples for acidity.

Styrofoam egg cartons are suggested here, if you do not have standard reaction trays. Because styrofoam has a chemically adverse effect on the ozone layer and is not biodegradable, its continued use to package products is in itself an important environmental issue. We are of course aware of this, and some students may raise this issue in class. Utilizing styrofoam egg cartons for activity-based science is at least one good way to make continued use of them. In some locations, egg cartons or similar containers made of other kinds of plastic may be available. If you have other ideas that use inexpensive and accessible materials or equipment, the GEMS project would welcome hearing about them.

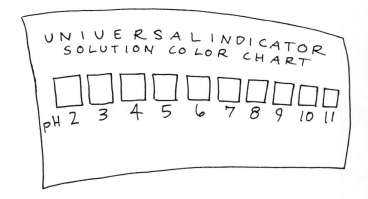

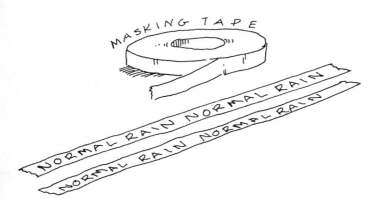

2. Label Containers

● Duplicate labels onto blank sheets of self-adhesive mailing labels using the master label sheets located at the back of this guide, or, use a permanent marker and masking tape to make your own labels. To make masking tape labels quickly: stick a length of masking tape several feet long onto a flat, smooth, surface; write the name of the solution several times along the strip; remove the tape from the table, segment by segment; and stick the labels on the containers.

● Label plastic cups with the name of each solution ("Tap Water," "Normal Rain," "Lemon Juice," "Vinegar," and "Baking Soda Solution"). You'll need to label one of each of these cups for each group of four students.

● Label one very small squeeze bottle, "Universal Indicator" for each group of four students.

● If there is no sink in your teaching area, label one or two large squeeze bottles, "Water" and set them near one or two buckets as rinse stations.

3. Prepare Solutions

You may want to have some other common acids and bases on hand for you or your students to test, if time permits.

● To prepare 500 mls of **baking soda solution:** dissolve approximately four tablespoons of baking soda in 500 milliliters of tap water. **Let the mixture sit overnight.**

● Use distilled water as **normal rain.** Normal rain water has the approximate pH of distilled water, as both are "pure" water with some carbon dioxide dissolved in it.

Other solutions (vinegar, lemon juice, tap water) do not require preparation.

4. Fill Labeled Squeeze Bottles

- Fill the very small squeeze bottles with Universal Indicator solution.

- If you have no sink, fill the large squeeze bottles with tap water.

All other solutions used in this session will be poured into labeled cups on the day of the activity.

5. Copy Data Sheet. Duplicate one pH data sheet for each pair of students from the master on page 38.

6. Make pH Chart. On a long sheet of butcher paper (5 to 10 feet in length), draw a pH scale, from 0 to 14. Write "very acidic," "slightly acidic," "neutral," "slightly basic," and "very basic" at appropriate places along the chart. We have found the following format for the pH scale to be most useful, as each group of students can record their results directly onto it:

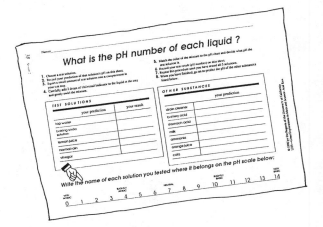

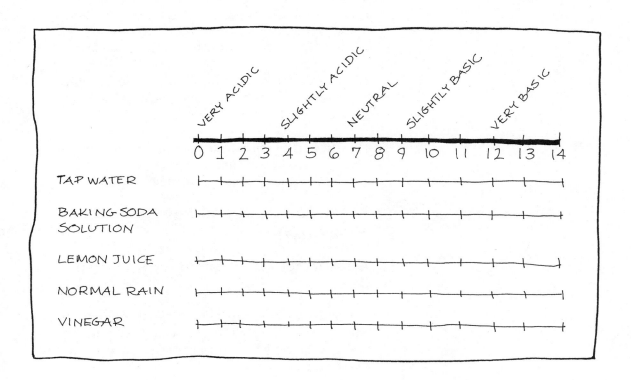

On the Day of the Activity

1. Set out one tray for each group of four students. On each tray, place one labeled cup for each of the five solutions (vinegar, lemon juice, baking soda solution, tap water, and normal rain). Fill all cups about one-third-full with the appropriate solution, and put one medicine dropper in each cup. On these same trays, place one small squeeze bottle of Universal Indicator solution, one Universal Indicator color chart, 2 egg cartons, and 2 data sheets. Do not distribute the trays at the beginning of the session. Instead, set them up at a place in the classroom where you can hand them out or have designated students from each working group pick them up.

2. Put safety goggles (if you are using them) in a central location.

3. Place several drinking straws and two cups half-filled with distilled water in the area where you plan to conduct the demonstration showing the acidity of normal rain.

4. Post the butcher paper pH scale on a wall in the classroom where it can remain throughout the session (and throughout the unit, if possible).

5. Arrange the room by pushing desks together or moving tables so there is one flat work area for each group of four students.

6. If there is no sink in the room, set up two empty buckets and one or two large squeeze bottles filled with water as a rinse station.

What's an Acid and How Do You Measure It?

Acids in Your Life: Introduce Acids and Bases

1. Have your students take out their homework sheets. Ask them to tell you what they found at home or at the grocery store. You may want to list these on the board.

2. Explain that "acid" is the general name for a whole group of chemicals that behave in similar ways. Ask what similarities they think this group of chemicals might have. [Common student responses often include: acid melts your skin, it eats through metal, it can dissolve stone. Some students mention "acid-washed" jeans, in which the color of the clothing dye is changed.]

3. Point out some of the shared properties of acids: they taste sour, break up proteins, dissolve metals, conduct electricity.

4. Ask for students to raise their hands if they have heard of chemicals called "bases." On the board, list some of the bases commonly used at home. [Baking soda, soap, toothpaste, ammonia, drain cleaner, other strong cleaners, milk of magnesia]

5. Explain that chemists classify chemicals into three groups according to how they react: those which are *acids* (or acidic), those which are *bases* (basic or alkaline), and those which are neither, called *neutral*. Chemicals that are acids all react in similar ways in certain situations. Chemicals that are bases also all react in similar ways to one another, but in different ways than acids.

Introduce the pH Scale

1. Explain that not all acids are the same strength. Some are very strong, some are moderate in their effects, and some are very weak. Focus the students' on the list of acids on the board and invite them to give examples of weak and strong acids. [*Weak acids:* carbonated beverages, tomatoes, orange juice, coffee, tea, vitamin C tablets. *Strong acids:* battery acid, toilet bowl cleaner, and certain strong cleaners]

2. Explain that scientists use a scale or a line that goes from 0—14, called the "pH scale," to classify how strong or weak an acid is. Ask students to indicate if they've heard of "pH" before (often students have seen pH referred to on shampoo or deodorant containers).

3. Refer to the large pH scale taped to the wall, on which you will construct a chart showing the results of the students' experimental investigations. Point out that acids are substances that have a pH of less than 7. Bases are substances with a pH greater than 7.

4. Ask the class what they suppose a substance is with a pH of exactly 7. [neutral] The lower the pH number, the stronger or more concentrated the acid. The higher the pH number, the stronger or more concentrated the base.

Introduce the Challenge: Investigating Acids and Bases

1. Tell the class that today they'll be testing a variety of substances, to see where they belong on the pH scale. To do this, they'll be using a liquid called Universal Indicator solution. Universal Indicator solution is one of a number of tools that chemists use to determine whether a substance is an acid or a base, and how acidic or basic it is.

2. At this point, you may want to review safety guidelines with the class, including what they should do if they get a chemical in their eyes, or on their skin or clothes. [Rinse it repeatedly with water] Reassure them that there are no really dangerous chemicals used in the class tests, but they should take careful precautions anyway, just as scientists do.

3. Demonstrate the procedure that each group will use to determine the pH of the substances:

> a. If you plan to use safety goggles, put them on first and show the class how to put them on. Although the solutions are not especially dangerous, some states require the use of goggles and teachers who have them available may wish to model chemical safety measures through their use.

> b. Choose a chemical to test, from those in the labelled cups. (Explain what the test solutions are and clarify what "baking soda" is by asking students where this substance is used at home.)

c. Before testing the substance, record a *prediction* of the pH of that substance on the data sheet.

d. Use a medicine dropper to add a small amount of the test solution into a compartment in the test tray.

e. Carefully add two drops of Universal Indicator solution to the test solution in the tray and gently swirl the mixture. (Make sure to caution students that Universal Indicator solution stains skin and clothes, so they should be careful not to spill or splash it.)

f. Compare the color of the mixture to the colors on the pH color chart and decide the pH of the test substance. (Explain that if the color is in between two of those shown on the chart, the students should choose a number that is in between, such as "5.5".)

g. Record your test result (pH number) on the data sheet.

4. Ask the class if they have any questions about the procedure. Remind them that the exact amount of test solution they use is not important, but they should try to use about the same amount for each test.

5. After they have made their predictions, tested, and recorded the pH of all of the solutions, they should write the names of each test solution at the appropriate place at the bottom of the data sheet, along the pH scale from 0–14.

6. Remind the class once more about being careful with chemicals and, if they are using goggles, to put on them on. Depending on the experience of the class, you may want to have them briefly repeat the steps of the testing procedure to you (or summarize the steps on the board). Remind them that each of them should make a prediction about the pH of each solution **before** testing it.

7. Explain that students will share equipment in groups of four, but teams of two within each group will conduct the experiments. Designate one student from each foursome to collect a tray of equipment.

Students Conduct the Tests

1. Have the students begin predicting and testing. Circulate around the room as needed, to make sure the procedure is understood and being followed, and to answer questions.

Note: If students find that the color of the test solution is too dark or cloudy after the Universal Indicator solution is added, have them add a little more of the test solution (this can be a problem with the juice test in particular). If the color is too faint, have them add more Universal Indicator solution.

2. If some groups finish their testing before others, direct them to the "other predictions" list on the data sheet, and encourage them to predict whether the other common substances listed there are acids, bases, or neutral, and what their pH's might be. Students should write their predictions in the space provided on the sheet.

3. Ask the students not to mix their chemicals together when they have finished their investigations (this can form part of an extension activity later on in the class, if there is extra time). If they have egg cartons with lids, ask them to close them, and, in any case, to set their equipment aside once they have finished the tests, and focus on making predictions of pH for the other common chemicals listed on the data sheet.

Pool Data from Groups

1. As each of the groups finishes the tests, have one student record their team's data for each test solution by marking the appropriate line on the butcher paper pH scale

2. If students still have equipment on their desks, have them set it aside now. It will not be needed further in this session. Focus their attention on the results recorded on the pH scale.

3. There is likely to be a range of pH's recorded by different groups for each test solution. Ask the students why different people might get different results after doing the same test on the same chemical. [Different amounts of chemical, different interpretations of color, contaminated medicine droppers, etc.] Ask what they think scientists do when they have disagreements about results. [Scientists discuss why they got different results; try to repeat each others' experiments exactly; design new experiments to focus on the differences.] Explain that the data on the chart represents the **range of results** the class obtained for each chemical.

4. You may want to ask the class for suggestions about how to interpret the range of data, using this first set of results as an example. Students may suggest: simply noting the whole range, from highest to lowest, calculating the average result, or determining the most common result (the mode). You could decide to use any of these methods to summarize the results.

5. When all results have been posted, ask the class which of the test solutions are acids. Note these on the pH chart, for instance by putting an "A" next to them. (You may need to emphasize that something is acidic if it has a **low** pH.) Ask which liquids were bases and record these on the chart with a "B." Finally, ask which of the test liquids seemed pretty close to neutral and place an "N" next to them.

If you do not think it is a good idea for your students to record their pH results directly onto the class pH scale, you can quickly get them to indicate what the result is for each solution in each student pair, by using numbered cards. To make a set of pH number cards (you will need one set for each pair of students), proceed as follows: Using a marker, write the numbers 0-14 and the number ½ on small index cards. Put all the cards in an envelope to make one set (15 cards in all). Distribute sets of reporting cards to each group, on the tray with the other equipment. Then, each group, when called on, can report the pH number they determined for each test chemical by designating one person to hold up a number card with the appropriate pH on it. If the pH is midway between two numbers, a "½ card" can be held up in the other hand.

6. Then ask several different students to report the pH's they predicted for the other common substances listed on their results data sheet. After each set of guesses, tell them what scientists have found to be the usual pH for that substance, and have the class decide whether it is very acidic, slightly acidic, very basic, slightly basic, or neutral. Record the results for these substances on the chart.

Note: The pH of each of the other common substances listed on the data sheet is:

battery acid—pH 1	drain cleaner—pH 13
cola—pH 4	ammonia—pH 11
milk—pH 6.5	stomach acid—pH 1
orange juice—pH 5	
(depending on the oranges)	

pH is a Logarithmic Scale

1. Refer to the pH chart and explain that the pH scale is a logarithmic scale, meaning that a substance of pH 6 is 10 times more acid than a substance of pH 7. (Please see the "Behind the Scenes" section on page 126 for more information on the pH scale.)

2. A useful comparison can be made using tap water (if it is around pH 7), by pointing out that substances with pH 6 are ten times more acidic than tap water; substances with pH 5 are one hundred times more acidic than tap water, and so on. The same applies to bases.

3. You could write these multiples in on the chart, above the appropriate pH (i.e., 10 X ACIDIC, 100 X ACIDIC, etc.) You might want to ask how much more acidic a substance of pH 4 is than one with a pH of 7, or how much more acidic pH 4 is than pH 6, or similar questions, to check your students understanding of this concept.

Another logarithmic scale that is useful to make comparisons with is the Richter scale, which measures the amount of ground movement in an earthquake. For example, a tremor of 5.0 on the Richter scale is ten times more powerful than one measured at 4.0.

What's the pH of Rain?

The pH of Normal Rain

1. From the class results, focus on the pH of normal rain water. Ask the students to suggest why rain water is slightly acidic, as compared with "pure water." Explain that while "pure water" should have a pH of 7.0, this can change, depending on what else the water contacts.

2. Give a demonstration of the acidifying effect of air on water, as follows:

   a. Show the class the two cups of "rain" water (distilled water) you have set aside. Add a generous squirt of Universal Indicator solution in one cup and ask a student to determine the pH. (You may need to hold the cup against a white background to help students see the color of the indicator from their seats.) Emphasize that the "rain" water in the two cups is exactly the same.

   b. Have another student blow out through a straw for fifteen seconds, into the water in the other cup, thereby adding carbon dioxide (and very roughly modeling rain falling through carbon dioxide in the atmosphere). Have the rest of the class count to 15 while the student blows through the straw. Tell the student that it's fine to take more than one breath while blowing.

   c. Add a squirt of Universal Indicator solution to the cup the student has blown into and have another student determine its pH.

   Note: For safety reasons, do **NOT** add the Universal Indicator solution to the water until after the student has blown into it.

d. You may want to ask questions like, "What change took place in the water?" [It became more acidic.] "Does anyone have any ideas about why this took place?" "What is in the air we breathe out that might cause water to change in this way?" Point out that when carbon dioxide gas dissolves in water and reacts with it, it becomes acidic. Breath blown out of the lungs has a higher carbon dioxide content than the normal air that the water has already had a chance to mix with, which explains the increase in acidity of the water with breath bubbled through it. The particular acid that is formed in this way is called carbonic acid.

3. Explain that, in a similar way, as pure water rains down through the sky, it mixes with some of the gases in air, such as carbon dioxide, and becomes acidic. Rain also naturally cleans the air as it falls, washing down dust particles suspended in the air. Point out that this small amount of acidity in rain water is good. Normal rain of pH 5.6 is acid enough to react with minerals from rocks and soils so they dissolve. These important minerals trickle down to nourish the roots of plants.

4. Record the range of normal rain as 5.6–6.0 on the class pH chart. Explain that, while normal rain water is slightly acidic, it is **not** what is referred to as "acid rain." You may want to emphasize this latter point to make sure your students understand it. You may also want to mention that rain water also dissolves oxygen from the air, and while this does not make water more acidic, oxygen is a very useful substance for organisms living in lake water, such as the lake and stream animals discussed later in the unit.

The pH Range of Acid Rain

1. Point out that **acid rain has been defined by scientists as rain with a pH of anything below about pH 5.6.**

2. Explain that acid rain is formed when the atmosphere is filled with gases and particles that come from factories, power-generating plants, and cars. These human-made pollutants in the air react with sunlight and moisture to form acids. These acids dissolve into the rainwater as it falls, and make it more acidic than carbon dioxide by itself does. How *acid* the rain becomes as it falls depends on how much of each of these pollutants there are.

3. Mark the acid rain range of pH 5.6 to pH 2.0 on the class chart.

Neutralization and Buffers

1. Ask the students what they think the resulting pH would be if equal amounts of substances of pH 3 and pH 9 are mixed together. [The pH of the resulting solution will fall somewhere between 3 and 9, but not necessarily exactly midway between. See note below.] Explain to the class that when an acid is mixed with a base, the two substances are said to *neutralize* each other.

Note: The final pH of a mixture of an acid and a base depends on the particular characteristics of the specific acid and base used. Not all acids and bases respond to neutralizing effects to the same extent. See the "Behind the Scenes" section at the end of this guide or a standard chemistry text for further detail.

2. You may want to introduce *buffers* by explaining that, like bases, they alter the pH of acids. However, instead of just moving the pH along the scale towards the "14" or base end, (point to the class pH scale) buffers are special chemicals that move the pH to a *fixed point* on the scale. Buffers are used to stabilize pH in solutions. (See the "Behind the Scenes" section at the end of this guide for more detailed explanations of neutralization and buffers.)

If there is time, as a demonstration, have two students choose two chemicals that they tested earlier (an acid and a base). Let the class predict the resultant pH if equal parts of these two chemicals were mixed, and then have the two volunteers conduct the test to see what happens. Alternatively, if the class is excited about testing substances for pH, and mixing them together to see what happens, you may wish to introduce an extra lesson to cover these activities, including some of the others suggested in the "Going Further" section at the end of this session.

You may also want to encourage students to experiment further with this procedure, for example, by having them add an antacid tablet (buffer) to one of their test solutions, and leaving it overnight to see how the pH changes. (They can crush the tablet between their fingers or just drop it in and have it dissolve overnight.) These and other activities are outlined more fully in the "Going Further" section at the end of this session.

Going Further

Testing Other Acids and Bases

If your students enjoyed the activities that explore acids and bases in Session 2, you may want to extend this activity. One way is to have your students test the pH of other substances, using Universal Indicator solution, to establish which are acids or bases. The names of substances containing acids at home, compiled by students in the homework activity after Session 1, would be a useful starting list, as would some of those substances listed under "Other Predictions" on the data sheet for Session 2. You may also want to include other substances that the students think might be interesting to test, provided you determine these substances to be safe.

Exploring Neutralization

If there is time in Session 2, or as an extra lesson, you could have each group of students choose two chemicals they tested earlier (an acid and a base), and have them predict what the resultant pH would be if equal parts of these two chemicals were mixed. Have them conduct the test, then discuss the class results. Students should find that different acids and bases, being different strengths, will produce different pH values when mixed together. Additionally, students could add a series of different volumes of an acid to a set volume of base, to observe the progressive effect of neutralization. Challenge them to determine by investigation exactly how much baking soda solution will be needed to neutralize a given amount of vinegar, lemon juice, or normal rain.

What's a Buffer and How Does It Work?

Have the students test the effects of buffers for themselves by adding an antacid tablet to a given (small) volume of vinegar. Challenge them to investigate whether adding more buffer (antacid) will further change the pH. You may want to discuss the purpose of buffers as chemicals that stabilize pH in solutions. You may also want to have students experiment further, for example, by adding buffer to some of their basic solutions, and then testing the pH with indicator. You could also have students compare the effects of various buffers (Tums®, Rolaids®, Alka-Seltzer®, etc.) on the pH's of some of the acid and base solutions they've already used, to see how their buffering properties differ.

Logarithmic Model

Demonstrate the "expanding" or exponential nature of the pH scale by having students each hold a card designating an acidic pH from 7 to 0, and form a line that represents a linear pH scale, on the acidic side, from 7 down to 0 (i.e. all students standing equidistant from one another). Then, with the student holding the "pH 7" card as a reference, have other students in the pH line move a distance away from the pH 7 reference place, according to how much more acidic they are. Thus, if the pH 6 student is ten centimeters away from the pH 7 student, the pH 5 student will have to be one hundred centimeters away, and so on. Obviously, it becomes impossible to continue this model past the first few numbers due to the distance requirements, so you may want to have your students just imagine where each one would have to stand. Or, you may want to assemble the class at an appropriate area outside on the school grounds, so students can attempt to graphically demonstrate the logarithmic nature of the pH scale.

What is the pH number of each liquid ?

1. Choose a test solution.
2. Record your prediction of that solution's pH on this sheet.
3. Squirt a small amount of test solution into a compartment in your test tray.
4. Carefully add 2 drops of Universal Indicator to the liquid in the tray and gently swirl the mixture.
5. Match the color of the mixture to the pH chart and decide what pH the test solution is.
6. Record your test result (pH number) on this sheet.
7. Repeat this procedure until you have tested all 5 solutions.
8. When you have finished, go on to predict the pH of the other substances listed below.

TEST SOLUTIONS

	your prediction	your result
tap water		
baking soda solution		
lemon juice		
normal rain		
vinegar		

OTHER SUBSTANCES

	your prediction
drain cleaner	
battery acid	
stomach acid	
milk	
ammonia	
orange juice	
cola	

Write the name of each solution you tested where it belongs on the pH scale below:

VERY ACIDIC				SLIGHTLY ACIDIC			NEUTRAL			SLIGHTLY BASIC			VERY BASIC
0	1	2	3	4	5	6	7	8	9	10	11	12	13	14

Session 3: Startling Statements About Acid Rain

Overview

n this session, your students play a game called "startling statements." In this game, students guess answers to key questions about acid rain, then compare their preconceptions with current scientific knowledge.

The process of "guesstimating" challenges students to think about their knowledge of the issues raised by the key questions. Many of the "startling statement" questions chosen for inclusion have an "answer" far outside of the expectations of the students, and therefore have some "shock" value, so students become doubly interested in finding out about them.

*And Now It's Time For . . .
Startling Statements!*

*Different classes and age levels may have
different initial reactions to the "game"
nature of the activity. A ninth-grade class
may not at first consider it "cool," while the
enthusiasm of some seventh graders can
occasionally go a bit overboard. We've found
that once the activity is underway, both
extremes tend to become involved in a
highly motivating and educational way. You
know your classes best, and may want to
introduce this approach somewhat
differently to different groups. Some
teachers have chosen to place this session in
a TV "game show" format, with themselves
as the host, beginning with the usual
dramatic flourish — "welcome ladies and
gentlemen to the game show that tells you
everything you wanted to know about acid
rain and more . . . yes . . . that's right . . .
it's time for Startling Statements . . . I'm
your host, and to start today's game . . . "*

The purposes of the activity are to: (1)
introduce information about acid rain in an
enjoyable and compelling way; (2) encourage
students to begin their explorations in science
with their own questions; and (3) enable students,
through questions and discussion, to synthesize
important information about socially relevant
scientific issues, and draw more confidently on
this assimilated information in subsequent
discussions.

This "Starting Statements" activity can be
greatly enhanced if you have additional
background knowledge to highlight the issues
brought out by the game and to enrich the
discussions that follow. If you haven't read the
background information included in "Behind the
Scenes" on page 123, we encourage you to do so
now. The "Resources" section, on page 142,
contains a list of other references, as of the
publication date of this guide. Of course, if you
have time, it's also helpful to read more recent
articles on the topic. Acid rain is a relatively new
area of scientific and social investigation, so
knowledge about, understanding of, and possible
solutions to the problems are likely to change
frequently. We remind you that newspaper/
magazine searches by students before and during
the unit are likely be one of your most valuable
sources of information.

What You Need

For the class:
- [ ] about 30 meters of cotton string or acrylic yarn
- [ ] a single-hole punch
- [ ] about 20 sheets of 8½" x 11" card stock
- [ ] 8 different "Startling Statements" (masters included, pages 50–53)

For each student:
- [ ] 1 copy of the article, "Pollution, Acid Rain, and You" (master included, page 49)

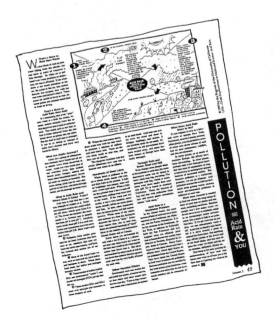

Getting Ready

Before the Day of the Activity

1. Make one "Startling Statement" card that can be worn as a necklace-type sign for each student:

a. Duplicate the "Startling Statements" onto card stock. The masters for the eight different startling statements are on pages 50–53, two to a page. Make enough copies of each of the eight statements so each student in your class has one "Startling Statement" card (i.e., several students will each wear a copy of the same "Startling Statement").

b. Use a paper cutter to cut the copies so each statement is on a half sheet.

c. With a paper punch, punch holes in the top two corners of each half sheet.

d. Cut a length of string several feet long, string it through the two holes, and tie it to make a necklace-type sign that can be worn around the neck. Repeat until you have made one sign for each student.

e. Make up a code for each "Startling Statement," and indicate this in some **small** way on each card (you might choose shapes, and draw small squares on all of the cards with one statement; triangles on all of the cards with another statement; etc., or you might use dots of different colors to stick on or mark with a marking pen). Make sure that these markings are not too obvious, as part of the value of the exercise is lost if too many students realize that other students have the same questions as they do (which allows them to know the question on their own back before trying to deduce what it is from the "guesstimates" of others).

f. Jot down the code for each "Startling Statement" on the "Scientific Responses to the Startling Statement Questions" on pages 50–53.

During which season are the rains most acidic?

We encourage you to make up other startling statements from your own reading and background knowledge of the subject. Some teachers find that the activity runs better with more than eight statements. However, if you choose to use more than eight, be aware that this significantly increases discussion time in the second half of the session. Too many statements, however interesting they may be in themselves, may contribute to making the activity repetitive or boring because it goes on for too long. But given these provisos, it may well make sense for you to add or adjust startling statements as they fit the interests of you and your class, or on particular emphases you've planned for this unit in relation to other curricular themes.

If you don't have the resources to give everyone a sign, you can still play the game. Give students without signs the job of making sure that students with signs obtain at least five answers to their questions.

2. Duplicate one copy of the article, "Pollution, Acid Rain, and You" for each student (master included, page 49).

On the Day of the Activity

If you do not already have the statements and questions from Session 1, and the pH scale from Session 2, posted in the classroom, put them up before this session. If possible, keep them posted for the rest of the unit, for easy reference.

➤ What Have We Discovered So Far?

1. Refer to the class pH chart on the classroom wall, and use it as a basis for questioning students about concepts covered so far in the unit, asking questions such as: "Which is more acidic—lemon juice or vinegar?" "What is the usual pH of rainwater, and why is it slightly acidic?" and "What is the pH range of acid rain?"

2. Post the statements and questions the class listed in Session 1. Ask the class to review these, and to point out any statements that need revision in light of information covered so far in the unit, and any questions that have been answered so far. (You may want to pick out particular questions and statements that you think need to be dealt with at this stage.) Out of the discussion, asterisk those questions that have been answered so far. (You may also want to re-write those student statements that need correction.)

The Startling Statements Game

Explain the Rules

1. Inform the class they are going to play a game about acid rain, called "Startling Statements." Explain the rules:

> a. In this game, all of you will wear a sign on your back. On the sign is a question. You will not know what the question on your sign is, but will find that out later. Part of the game is that you guess what the question you are wearing says.

You may decide to refer to the list of statements and questions at the beginning of every session during the unit, and to ask students each time which questions about acid rain they think they have covered, if they have any more questions, or if there is information they need to clarify or understand better. Be aware that if you decide to do this, you will need to adjust your entire time frame accordingly.

b. Each of you goes around the class, asking at least five people to first read your question **silently—without giving it away to you—** and then to answer it as best they can, by trying to guess what the answer to the question on your back is. Write down the five answers to your question on a piece of paper that you carry with you.

c. After you have asked at least five people what they think is the answer to your question, sit down and summarize the answers. If your answers were numbers, you might summarize as follows: "range from 2 to 5" or "average was 3." If your answers were not numbers, you might summarize as follows: "most people said California, one said New York, and one said Florida."

d. After you have written down your summary, then try to guess what the question on your back says (before you look at it!).

e. You may then look at your question, to see if your guess was correct.

f. After you finish, we will analyze each question, to see how your answers compare with those of other acid rain researchers.

2. Strongly emphasize that it is not expected that anyone who plays "Startling Statements" will actually know the complete and accurate answers to all or even most of the questions. Remind the class that this is a *game*—the main idea is to have fun by guessing what they think the answers are, then later to learn something by comparing their "guesstimates" with the findings of scientific researchers.

3. Ask the class if they have any questions about what to do. Make sure each student has a pen and piece of paper to write down the suggested answers. Then have the students line up, so you can "hang a question on them." One good way to do this is to call up small groups at a time, ask them to turn with their backs facing you, and hang different signs randomly, one on each student's back. After this is done, they can begin the game.

Analyze The Questions

1. When most students have finished collecting their answers, and are in the process of summarizing them, ask everyone to return to their seats. Remind them that, after they have made their summaries, they should guess what the question on their back is, **before** taking it off and looking at it. Give the students a few minutes more to complete their summaries.

2. Ask the first group of students *with the same question* to come to the front of the class. An easy way of doing this, and also to keep track of the "Scientific Responses" to each question, is to refer to the code you established for each question (e.g., "green triangles," "red dots," etc.). In this way, you can simply ask for the "green dot" questions to come to the front, and you can quickly look up your "green dot" scientific response (see "Getting Ready").

3. Have one student read aloud what the question was, and then ask each responding student in turn to report their summary of the class guesses. If you find that students have had difficulties in summarizing their answers, get them to list each answer, and then ask a volunteer from the class to attempt a summary.

4. When the students have finished reporting, ask the class if they have any other comments or thoughts about why a certain answer might be accurate. Read out the "Scientific Responses." Be sure to include any questions or points of discussion you think relevant. Your students may also have other questions or issues that arise from this new information. The "Scientific Responses" are listed for you at the end of this activity, but you are encouraged to add your own information (and to make up your own startling statements more relevant to your class, for that matter!). Continue getting reports from each group of students with the same question, followed by the appropriate "Scientific Responses" and discussion, until each group has had a chance to report back.

Note: Be careful to avoid the temptation to over-emphasize the "Scientific Responses," and end up turning the session into a theoretical discourse by yourself on the "facts" about acid rain. This session is meant only as an stimulating introduction to some of the important background information about acid rain. There will be ample time in later sessions, and through the homework reading assignments, to introduce more detailed information needed to prepare for the town meeting in the final session. As a rule, let student questions and statements lead the discussion arising out of the startling statements, and pace the discussion according to the interest level of the class in each question. Above all, don't swamp them with too much information at once.

So, What Have We Learned?

1. Refer to the list of student statements and questions from Session 1. Just as at the beginning of this "Startling Statements" activity, ask the class if there are any statements they would now like to modify or extend, and any questions they think have been answered. Ask students if they have any new questions to add.

2. Encourage the class to keep adding to what they know about acid rain, and to keep sorting through the information they come across, to make sure they understand it. Remind the class that this sorting of information, and re-evaluation of what is understood, is something scientists do constantly.

Homework Reading Assignment

1. Hand out the reading assignment on acid rain. This gives students a written version of the important concepts about acid rain covered so far in the unit and some additional information.

2. Point out that, later in the unit, each student will represent a local interest group at a town meeting called to consider what to do about the effects of acid rain on a lakeside town and its surrounding environment. For this town meeting, each student will need to have a good understanding of how acid rain forms, and what effects it has. This is one reason to read the homework article carefully.

3. Reveal that in the next session they will be doing an experiment to model what happens to a lake when it is exposed to acid rain. They also will be looking at some of the possible ways of treating a lake after it becomes highly acidic.

Scientific Responses to the Startling Statement Questions

Where in the United States is the problem of acid rain the worst?

ANSWER: The area most affected in the U.S. is in the Northeast, where the pH of *average* rainfall is 4.0–4.5. Individual storms as low as 3.0–4.0 are not unusual. Values less than 3.0 have been found. The area in the country where there seems to be the most rapid increase in acid precipitation is the Southeast. West of the Mississippi River the problem is generally not as severe, with certain exceptions, including the Los Angeles Basin, the San Francisco Bay Area, Colorado, and a number of other places.

What proportion of the lakes at high elevations in the Adirondack Mountains (in upstate New York) are so acid that they have a pH below 5.0?

ANSWER: More than half. Of these lakes, 90% are so acidic that they contain no fish! Compare this with the same lakes from 1924–1937: only 4% had a pH under 5.0 or could support no fish.

What is the pH of the most acid rainstorm every measured?

ANSWER: 2.4.—This storm took place in Scotland in 1970.

In the greater Los Angeles area the pH of the fog has been as acid as . . .

ANSWER: 2.0—Acid fog can be even more acidic than acid rain. One reason why trees and plants at high altitudes are so severely affected by acid rain is that they are often exposed to highly acidic fog or mist. This has the effect of constantly bathing the leaves and other parts of the trees and plants in acid.

Oxides of sulfur (SOx) and oxides of nitrogen (NOx) in our air form acid rain. How many miles can these pollutants travel from place to place?

ANSWER: Depending on wind speed, direction, and duration, SOx and NOx can travel across continents, oceans, and international boundaries, for hundreds and even thousands of miles. Gaseous pollutants can stay aloft for up to four days or even longer. Another factor affecting how far the pollutants travel is the height at which they are deposited into the atmosphere. The tallest smoke stacks can deposit the pollutants high in the atmosphere, where they get carried long distances by the jet stream and other powerful winds.

During which season are rains the most acidic?

ANSWER: Summer rains are often the most acidic. While this does not always occur, there are several reasons why it is often the case:
1) It typically rains less often in the summer. The longer between each rain, the more air pollutants collect in the atmosphere before they are washed down to earth as acid rain.
2) There is often less air circulation in the summer so pollutants are not dispersed by wind.
3) There tends to be increased automobile use in the summer time, leading to increased emissions of NO_x, and some SO_x, compounds.
4) There is often increased use of electricity for air conditioning, and the power plants that produce electricity burn coal or oil, which contributes to acid rain.

What % of the pollution that causes acid rain comes from the Northern Hemisphere? the Southern Hemisphere?

ANSWER: Northern Hemisphere 93%/Southern Hemisphere 7%. Most of the heavily industrialized countries are located in the Northern Hemisphere, for example the United States, the European nations, and Japan.

What can be done to make lakes less acid?

Answer: A lot of information about exactly how acid rain causes damage has not yet been sufficiently explained, so one thing that needs doing urgently is scientific research. More is known about the effects of acid rain on lakes and streams than its effects on forests. Lakes affected by acid rain can sometimes be treated by chemicals called buffers, which neutralize the acid, but as long as acid rain water continues to enter the lakes, more buffer has to be added. Obviously the best way to fix acid rain is to control its sources, i.e., emissions from factories and cars, and from house heating fuels. Tall chimneys don't really work, because the SO_x and NO_x, which cause acid rain, are just distributed over a wider area. We could develop expensive ways of taking SO_x and NO_x out of these emissions, or we could use these fuels less, for instance by developing other sources of energy, such as solar energy.

There's More to Rain than Water

We may think of rain as pure water falling from the clouds, but rain takes in some of whatever it falls through. So when air is polluted with waste products or chemicals, the rain is affected. Even when there is not much pollution in the air, the gases in the air, like carbon dioxide and oxygen, mix with the rain water and dissolve into it. These gases are useful to have in rain, because plants and animals need them to keep on living.

There's More to Acid Rain than Acid

It's interesting that even "pure" rain water is a little bit acidic, because carbon dioxide from the air that dissolves into it makes carbonic acid. This much acid is not bad; in fact it helps minerals from the soil break down so plants can use them. But the acid in acid rain is stronger. It can be as strong as vinegar or toilet bowl cleaner and have very harmful effects.

What Are Acids Anyway?

Acids are a group of substances that chemists have found out all act in similar ways when dissolved in water. Acids are very much part of our everyday lives; they include lemon juice, vinegar, aspirin and many other household items. So not all acids are strong or harmful. But some strong acids can be very dangerous to our skin, can burn through metal, and do damage in other ways.

What Is Acid Rain and Where Does It Come From?

Acid rain is rain that has a certain strength of acidity in it. Scientists measure acidity on a scale called the pH scale, which goes from 0 to 14. The lower the number, the more acidic it is. Normal rain is usually between pH 6 and pH 7. Anything more acidic than pH 5.6 is acid rain. Some acid rainstorms are even more acidic than pH 3.0. Here's how acid rain forms:

❶ Pollution from smoke goes into the air from factories that burn coal or oil, smelters that turn ore from the earth into metals, and from the exhaust that comes out of car tailpipes.

❷ Most of the fossil fuels we use, such as coal and oil, have sulfur and nitrogen in them. When these fuels burn, the sulfur and nitrogen become oxides.

❸ These oxides of sulfur (called SOx and pronounced "socks") and oxides of nitrogen (NOx) go up into the air.

❹ These oxides (SOx and NOx) react with sunlight and moisture to form droplets of acid.

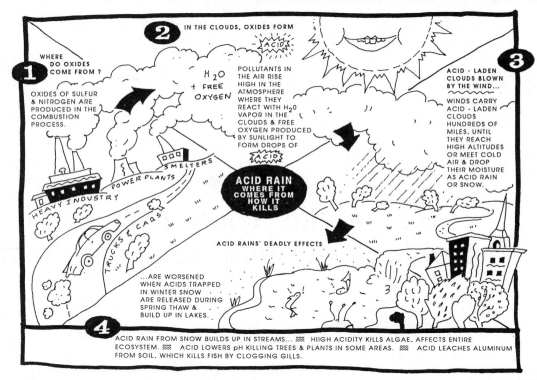

① WHERE DO OXIDES COME FROM? OXIDES OF SULFUR & NITROGEN ARE PRODUCED IN THE COMBUSTION PROCESS.

HEAVY INDUSTRY — POWER PLANTS — SMELTERS — TRUCKS & CARS

② IN THE CLOUDS, OXIDES FORM ACID H₂O + FREE OXYGEN POLLUTANTS IN THE AIR RISE HIGH IN THE ATMOSPHERE WHERE THEY REACT WITH H₂O VAPOR IN THE CLOUDS & FREE OXYGEN PRODUCED BY SUNLIGHT TO FORM DROPS OF ACID

③ ACID - LADEN CLOUDS BLOWN BY THE WIND... WINDS CARRY ACID - LADEN CLOUDS HUNDREDS OF MILES, UNTIL THEY REACH HIGH ALTITUDES OR MEET COLD AIR & DROP THEIR MOISTURE AS ACID RAIN OR SNOW.

ACID RAIN WHERE IT COMES FROM HOW IT KILLS

ACID RAINS' DEADLY EFFECTS

④ ...ARE WORSENED WHEN ACIDS TRAPPED IN WINTER SNOW ARE RELEASED DURING SPRING THAW & BUILD UP IN LAKES.

ACID RAIN FROM SNOW BUILDS UP IN STREAMS... ≈ HIGH ACIDITY KILLS ALGAE, AFFECTS ENTIRE ECOSYSTEM. ≈ ACID LOWERS pH KILLING TREES & PLANTS IN SOME AREAS. ≈ ACID LEACHES ALUMINUM FROM SOIL, WHICH KILLS FISH BY CLOGGING GILLS.

❺ When the rain comes down, these acids mix with the rain water to produce a solution of sulfuric acid and nitric acid. These are the two main acids in acid rain, and they can be deadly.

The diagram included with this article illustrates how acid rain is formed and some of its effects.

Hundreds of Dead Lakes

When there is pollution in the air it forms acids, mixes with rain, and then falls to the ground. It falls on buildings and people, trees and cars, rivers and lakes. When it falls on the ground near a lake it runs off into the lake, adding even more acid to the water. If the water gets too acidic, it has a very harmful, sometimes deadly effect on some plants and fish. In turn, other organisms that eat these plants and fish cannot survive. When most of the plants and animals in a lake die, biologists describe the lake as "dead." Scientists report that, due to acid rain, there are already hundreds of "dead" lakes in the eastern and midwestern United States and in Canada.

Some lakes are surrounded by soil with a lot of lime in it, a chemical that can help make the water in the lake less acidic even when highly acidic rain flows into it. But lakes surrounded by other kinds of soil do not have this natural defense against acid, and can be very badly affected by acid rain.

Other Harmful Effects

Sometimes acid rain makes the soil itself too acidic, or harms leaves, so that trees and other plants turn brown and die. Trees in high mountain areas may sometimes be bathed in an acid cloud. Acid rain can also eat away the metal and stone in bridges, buildings, and statues. It can produce spots on car paint. Inscriptions on old gravestones have been eroded away, and many historic statues in Europe have been badly damaged.

Through Rain and Snow, Sleet and Hail

Even though most people think of the problem as acid rain, the same destructive acids can be found in snow, sleet, hail, fog, and smog. The strongest acid fog, which is sometimes even more acidic than acid rain (pH 2!) is found in southern California. There, the mixture of fog and rain with pollutants from cars and power plants sometimes causes "acid smog."

Acid Rain is a Worldwide Problem

In the United States, the most serious effects of acid rain have been reported in the Northeast, the Mideast, and the Rocky Mountains. It is on the increase in the Southeast. In the West, in addition to Colorado, both the San Francisco and Los Angeles areas are affected. Acid rain is found all over the world, from Mexico to Sweden, England to Japan, India to Canada. Many Canadians are very upset about acid rain's effects there, which they blame on air pollution from the United States. They have asked the United States to find ways to reduce the pollution. Because pollution can be carried by the wind across great distances, even countries and areas that do not have much industry can be seriously affected.

What Does Acid Rain Mean to Me?

If you happen to live in a lakeside town in upstate New York, Minnesota, eastern Canada, or many other places, you are probably aware of some very direct effects of acid rain on your community, wildlife, and the environment.

In some places, as in much of northern Europe, the effects have been devastating. In other places, perhaps only a few biologists know that one type of salamander or frog is becoming an endangered species because of increased acidity. But because pollution is a worldwide problem, we are all affected. And pollution around the world has definitely been getting worse, causing many environmental problems in addition to acid rain.

Much more research is needed to find out about the long-range effects of acid rain on plants and animals, including ourselves. Because people don't live under water, we do not have to try to suddenly adapt to an increasingly acidic environment, like a plant or fish in an acidified lake. If we get acid rain on our skin, we can immediately wash it off. Acid rain is usually only harmful if it stays around a plant or animal for some time. But anything that affects plants at the lower end of the food chain, and that also affects the water we drink and the air we breathe, definitely affects us.

One thing is for sure: gaining an understanding of how acid rain forms and what its effects are is the first step in figuring out what to do about it. ≈

POLLUTION ≈ Acid Rain & YOU

Where in the United States is the problem of acid rain the worst?

What proportion of the lakes at high elevations in the Adirondack Mountains (in upstate New York) are so acid that they have a pH below 5.0?

What is the pH of the most acid
rainstorm ever measured?

In the greater Los Angeles area
the pH of the fog has been
as acid as...

Oxides of sulfur (SO_X) and oxides of nitrogen (NO_X) in our air form acid rain. How many miles can these pollutants travel from place to place?

During which season are rains the most acidic?

What % of the pollution that
causes acid rain comes from the
Northern Hemisphere?
the Southern Hemisphere?

What can be done
to make lakes less acid?

Session 4: Fake Lakes

Overview

In this activity, students investigate the pH of a simulated "lake," as it relates to the soil substrate that "surrounds" the lake and the rain water that enters the lake. To do this, they use the Universal Indicator technique they learned in Session 2.

First, a normal rainstorm rains on the soil that forms the substrate of the students' "lakes," and they determine the resultant pH of the "lake water." Students note the differences in pH between the lakes in different groups, due to the use of different soils to "surround" them. Then, an acid rainstorm (of pH 3) rains on their lakes. The students predict, then measure, the new pH of the "lake." Some of the soils used may have a natural buffering capacity, and therefore the simulated lakes "surrounded" by these soils don't become as acidic as one would expect. Finally, a buffer is added to the lakewater. Students observe firsthand how a buffer can neutralize the acid and bring the lake back to a "healthier" pH.

The purposes of this session are to: (1) review the concepts of acid, base, neutralization and buffer; (2) give students practice in using Universal Indicator solution to determine pH; (3) introduce the components of a lake system that contribute to, and are affected by, acidification by acid rain— in particular, to show how the acidity of lake water is affected by the interaction of soil substrate and acid precipitation; and (4) investigate one method suggested as a solution to lake acidification, which uses a buffer to neutralize the acid.

What You Need

For the class:

- [ ] 1 large sheet of butcher paper (for recording results and re-examining them in Session 5)
- [ ] 2 marking pens of different colors
- [ ] 3–4 liters of distilled water
- [ ] 1 milliliter (ml) of 1 molar (1M) sulfuric acid solution (See the "Resources" section on page 142 for information on how to purchase 1 molar sulfuric acid solution, and the "Behind the Scenes" section on page 123 for instructions on how to make a 1 molar solution from more concentrated sulfuric acid. See also page 56 for suggestions about what to do if sulfuric acid is unavailable.)
- [ ] 1 glass pipette or small graduated cylinder for measuring a 1 ml quantity of acid
- [ ] 1 two-liter container for mixing acid rain solution
- [ ] 1 pair of goggles
- [ ] several tablespoons of several different soil samples (See "Getting Ready" section for this session)
- [ ] 1 tablespoon
- [ ] approximately 10 Tums® tablets
- [ ] access to a sink (or 2 buckets, and 1 or 2 large squeeze bottles, such as empty dishwashing soap bottles, for a rinse station)

ROLL OF BUTCHER PAPER

8 CAFETERIA TRAYS

32 CLEAR PLASTIC CUPS

16 MEDIUM SQUEEZE BOTTLES

DISTILLED WATER

COFFEE FILTERS

SULFURIC ACID

8 20 ml GRADUATED CYLINDERS

TUMS

ABOUT 32 RUBBER BANDS

32 FAKE LAKE DATA SHEETS

32 WHITE PAPER

8 COLOR CHARTS

2 MARKERS

TABLESPOON

5 ZIPLOCK BAGS OF SOIL

8 SQUEEZE BOTTLES OF UNIVERSAL INDICATOR

GOGGLES

GLASS PIPETTE

A solution of sulfuric acid makes a fairly authentic facsimile of acid rain, as it is the most common type of acid that actually occurs in acid rain. If you don't have 1 molar sulfuric acid, it can be ordered and is readily available. See the "Resources" section on page 142 for ordering information. Ordered items can often be received in less than a week. If you have sulfuric acid in a more concentrated form than 1 molar, follow the instructions in "Behind the Scenes" on page 141, for diluting the acid to the proper concentration. If you are ready to conduct the activity tomorrow and have no way of obtaining sulfuric acid, you can use full-strength white distilled vinegar as acid rain. While vinegar will work to acidify the "fake lakes," there are reasons why vinegar is not a good substitute for acid rain. Vinegar is a solution of acetic acid. Acetic acid is a "weak" acid, while sulfuric is a "strong" acid. (See "Behind the Scenes" for a discussion of this terminology.) Even when the concentration of these two different acids is adjusted so they have the same pH, their characteristics are different enough for them to behave somewhat differently in a "lake." Vinegar should still provide some relative approximation of the main results, but may significantly reduce the accuracy of the fake lake simulation. Thus, vinegar should only be used when sulfuric acid cannot be obtained.

For each group of 4 students:
- ☐ 1 cafeteria tray
- ☐ 1 small squirt bottle of Universal Indicator solution (from Session 2)
- ☐ 1 Universal Indicator Color Chart (from Session 2)
- ☐ 2 medium squeeze bottles, approximately 150 to 300 ml (5–10 oz capacity)
- ☐ 1 graduated cylinder for measuring 20 ml quantities

For each student:
- ☐ 1 tall clear flexible plastic cup (9 oz. capacity)
- ☐ 1 coffee filter paper, basket-type, approximately 8 inches (20 cms) in full diameter (which the box label often describes as fitting into a basket/cup 3¼ inches in diameter). Common brands such as Safeway, Melitta, or Mr. Coffee, work well.
- ☐ 1 rubber band (to secure the filter paper when it is suspended across the top of the plastic cup)
- ☐ a sheet of white paper or other white background
- ☐ 1 "Acid Rain" data sheet (master included, page 71)
- ☐ (optional) 1 pair of safety goggles

Getting Ready

Before the Day of the Activity

1. **Label Containers.** Label 1 squeeze bottle, "Normal Rain" and 1 squeeze bottle "Acid Rain" for each group of four students. (See "Getting Ready" section in Session 1 for hints on making labels.)

2. **Prepare Solutions.**

   • Prepare 2 liters of **acid rain solution** by adding 1 ml of 1M sulfuric acid to two liters of distilled water. Always wear goggles when working with acid of 1 molar strength and use extreme care. Remember the adage when diluting acid: "Do as you oughter, add acid to water!"

● As in Session 2, the **normal rain** used in this activity will be distilled water. No additional preparation is necessary.

3. **Fill Labeled Squeeze Bottles.** Fill the newly-labeled acid rain and normal rain squeeze bottles.

4. **Acquire Soil Samples.** Detailed information on the methods for collecting an adequate range of soil samples is described in the "Behind the Scenes" section on page 123, including an "ideal" way and as "easy" way to collect soils. **THIS NEED NOT BE A MAJOR PROJECT.** You can start small and add to your soil collection as you present *Acid Rain* to subsequent classes. A small bag of soil can last for many presentations of the activity. Once you have a collection of soil samples, it is unlikely you will have to collect them again.

You will need to acquire small amounts of several different soils. While three different types of soils would be adequate, five or six are ideal. Depending on where you live and whether or not there are a wide variety of soil types nearby, it might be a very simple task to collect several different types practically from your own neighborhood. By enlisting student assistance, you can also collect appropriate soils from different backyards, parks, or trips to the beach. You may want to give the soils concise and easily-remembered names that may appeal to your students and/or in some way refer to soil composition or the place where they were found.

5. **Prepare Coffee Filters:** Provide enough coffee filters so there is one for each student in the class, and several to spare. Divide them equally into as many groups as the number of soil sample types you have. On the outer edge of the upper side of each coffee filter, write in pencil the name of the soil sample to be used in that filter (so that, when the filter is suspended in a plastic cup, with its edge overlapping the rim of the cup, and secured by a rubber band, the label you have written in pencil is easily readable).

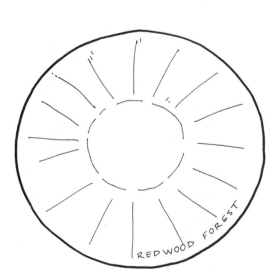

An 8-inch diameter square of paper towel will also work as a filter, but you first need to check that it does not have residual acid in it. To do this, run water through it and compare the pH of the water before and after. In addition, the paper towel does not hang as easily in the plastic cup, and may be more difficult for students to secure with a rubber band.

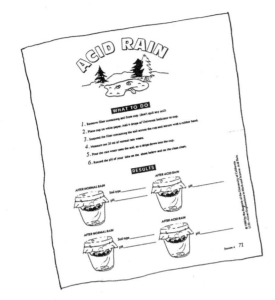

6. **Prepare Soil Samples:** Add a heaping tablespoon of the appropriate soil sample to each labeled coffee filter, and put the filter containing the soil into a clean 9 oz. plastic cup. These will be used by students to make the "fake lakes." Set aside the cups containing the filters and soil samples, ready to hand out in class.

7. **Duplicate Data Sheets.** Copy one "Acid Rain" data sheet for each student (master provided, page 71).

8. Hang the butcher paper in a convenient place on the classroom wall, for students to record the results of their "lake" experiments. Also post the large pH scale from Session 2.

The Day of the Activity

1. **Set out one tray for each group of four students.** On each tray place: four fake lakes (soil and coffee filter in a cup, each with a different soil), four rubber bands, four sheets of white paper, one small squeeze bottle of Universal Indicator solution, one Universal Indicator Color Chart, one squeeze bottle of normal rain, and four "Acid Rain" data sheets. Do not distribute these trays yet. Also set aside separately one squeeze bottle of "acid rain" per group.

2. **Arrange the room** by pushing desks together or moving tables so there is one flat work area for each group of four students.

3. If there is no sink in the room, set up two empty buckets and one or two large squeeze bottles filled with water as a rinse station.

Discussion of Homework Reading Assignment

1. Focus attention on the homework article, with the goal of generating a discussion that reviews some of the major concepts introduced so far in the unit. You might want to ask the following:

- What is the normal pH for rainwater, and why? Is this a problem?

- What is the pH range of acid rain? Why is this a problem?

- What is acid rain produced from and how is it formed?

- In which places is acid rain most commonly found?

2. Conclude the review by noting that burning coal in electricity generating plants, oil in household heaters, and gasoline in cars, all contribute to acid rain.

3. If your students have not raised the subject specifically, refer them to the diagram in the homework material that mentions oxides of sulfur and nitrogen. These were also referred to in the "Startling Statements" activity. Briefly review the concept that the main pollutants that produce acid rain are various mixtures of nitrogen and sulfur with oxygen (called oxides—NO, NO_2, and SO, SO_2, SO_3). Scientists call the nitrogen oxides, "NOx." (pronounced "nox" — rhymes with rocks) Ask the class: "What do you think they call sulfur oxides?" [SO_x] Explain that the NO_x reacts with sunlight and moisture to produce nitric acid. In the same way, SO_x reacts to produce sulfuric acid. These are the main acids in acid rain. You may want to draw a simple diagram on the board, including sun, clouds, cars, and factories to show how acid rain is formed.

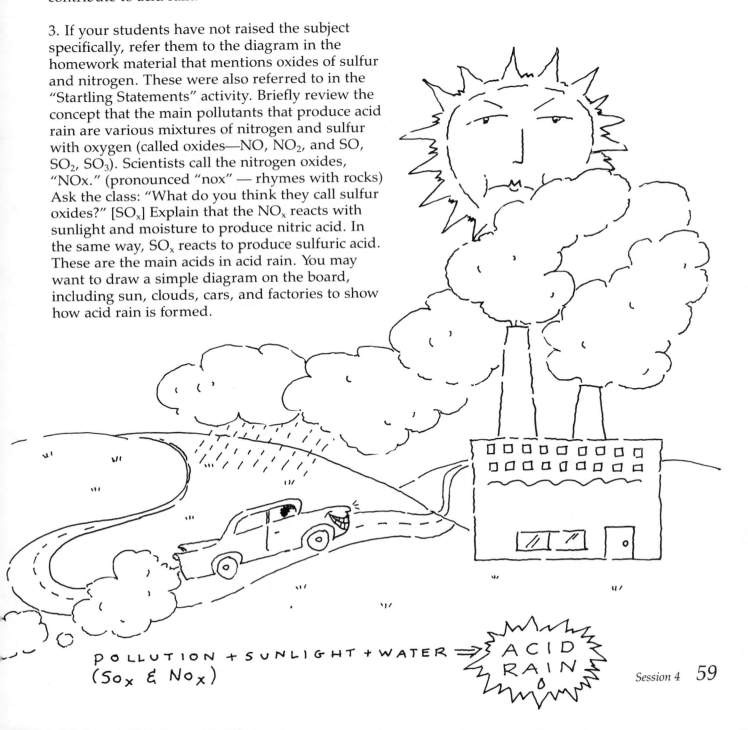

POLLUTION + SUNLIGHT + WATER ⇒ ACID RAIN
(SO_x & NO_x)

For more information on the possible effects of acid rain on human health, please also see the note on page 73.

Some experiments are underway to test lung responses to dilute acids in mist form. Little is known about the effects of acid rain on our skin and hair. Some of the potential secondary effects of acid rain are known to be extremely hazardous. For example, heavy metals, such as mercury in soil and lead and copper in pipes, can be dissolved by acidic water. If ingested at high enough levels, these heavy metals can have serious consequences for human health, and have been linked to cancer, brain damage, and other illnesses.

According to an article in New Scientist *(see "Resources" section for reference listing) "Acidified waters have a low pH, a low concentration of calcium and a high concentration of soluble aluminium leached from the soil. This combination is toxic to fish. Acid water disrupts the mechanisms by which fish maintain their balance of fluids, and they lose body salts, especially sodium. Newly hatched and very young fish are extremely sensitive. Fish lay fewer eggs in acid water and many of these eggs die. Aluminium in acid water damages the gills of fish; they become covered in mucus, and the fish suffocate."*

4. Point out that there are some possible and hopeful solutions to the acid rain problem, and that the class will begin talking about some of these today and in upcoming sessions. In the next two sessions, they will be taking on different roles and points of view to learn more about how all of us are affected by the problems caused by acid rain, and how we can take part in positive solutions.

The Effects of Acid Rain

1. Tell the class that in order to look at possible solutions, it is first necessary to be clear about the sorts of problems that acid rain causes and what its effects are.

2. Ask the class to review what the major effects of acid rain are and summarize these on the board. For example:

- Humans: much remains unknown about direct effects. It is important to note that virtually all damage caused by acid rain to the environment, food chain, and water supply also affects people.

- Plants/trees: especially harmful to plants at high altitudes, although more research needs to be done.

- Steel/iron/building materials: can be corroded.

- Statues/stone: can be eroded or eaten away.

- Paint finish on cars: can be corroded/marred/ruined.

- Aquatic life: affected the most because fish and aquatic plants must live in a continuously acidic environment.

3. You may want to add to your board diagram, showing the effects of acid rain on the environment.

If You Were a Fish. . . .

1. Explain that in this session, the class is going to look at lakes, as a special example of how acid rain can affect our environment.

2. Ask the students, "If you were a fish, what pH water would you like to live in? What pH's would you definitely not like to live in?" [Many students may respond with "14," the value farthest away from the acid end of the scale. Give this response merit as being one possible answer, but solicit other answers as well. Some students are likely to surmise that for a fish to live in an extremely basic environment is not so healthy either!]

3. You can also ask students, "What led you to that answer?" and discover their reasoning. If they seem baffled or unresponsive, ask them what kind of environment a fish lives in [Water]. Ask them, "What was the pH of the tap water samples we tested?" [around 6 to 8] Ask students what the normal pH of rain water is [around pH 5.6]. You might also point out that very basic environments can also be quite harmful, asking for example, "Would fish be able to live in Drano?"

4. Tell the class that research scientists have found that the safe zone for aquatic life is pH 5 through pH 9 (depending on how adapted each organism is to acid) and draw that range in on the class pH scale. Point out that sometimes adult fish, salamanders, frogs, and other animals can survive in a non-ideal pH, but often their eggs, larvae, and young cannot survive. Review the pH range for acid rain (pH 2 through pH 5.6) and note the difficulties for aquatic organisms exposed to this pH range. (You may want to remind students of the startling statement in Session 3 that told them: 90% of all lakes at high elevations in the Adirondack Mountains with a pH below 5.0 have no fish at all, due to acidification of the lakes.)

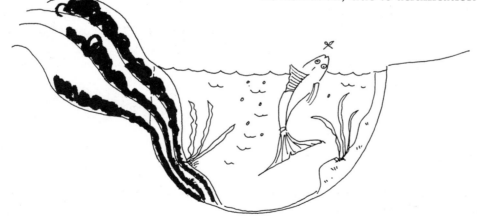

Anatomy of a Lake

1. Ask your students "What do we need in order to have a lake?" [water, fish, plant life, a hole in the ground, trees, shore, etc.] Draw each element very roughly on the board as they name it (leave the outline of the ground out, until they mention it, or until it becomes obvious that the lake needs one). When they get to the ground, ask them: "What kinds of things surround a lake? What does the ground around a lake consist of?" [soil, rocks, sand, dirt, animal and plant waste materials] Explain that it might be surprising to some of the class, but the substances in the ground around the lake also each have their own pH. Introduce the term *substrate*, to describe the ground and soil that lines the bottom of the lake, and that surrounds it.

2. You may want to follow this up by asking the class how this pH is formed. [Some of it comes from the chemicals in the rocks themselves, and some of it from the plant and animal remains that mix with the soil, and gets washed into the ground water.] Because the soil, sand, or rock around a lake have their own pH, they can affect the pH of the lake. Tell the class that they are now going to see for themselves how the different pH's of soils that surround lakes affect the pH of the lake water.

Experimenting with "Fake Lakes"

1. Explain that each pair of students will have two lakes. Different lakes will have different soils or substrates. First the students will observe the pH of their lake after a normal "rainstorm." Then an acid rainstorm will come and rain on their lakes. Finally, they will try an experimental method, which uses a special chemical called a *buffer*, to see if they can successfully treat the acid in their lakes.

You may want to have your students compare their lakes to a "control" lake—a lake containing 4 drops of Universal Indicator solution and 20 ml of normal rain. This will enable them to determine more exactly the effect of each substrate on the resultant pH of their fake lakes. However, because the experiment is a fairly primitive model of a situation in the natural world, such exactness is not necessary. The purpose of the simulation is to observe the gross effects of the variables of substrate and acid rain on lake pH.

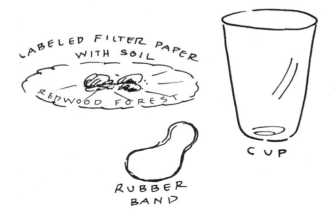

LABELED FILTER PAPER WITH SOIL

REDWOOD FOREST

CUP

RUBBER BAND

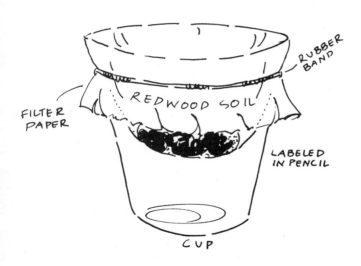

RUBBER BAND

FILTER PAPER

REDWOOD SOIL

LABELED IN PENCIL

CUP

You may want to demonstrate what the pH of the "rain" water is. Don't be surprised if it varies slightly, even from bottle to bottle in the class, because it will be affected in each case by how much it has mixed with the carbon dioxide in the air. This slight variability should not affect the results of the experiment in a major way, because the changes in pH caused by the different soil types are usually much greater.

2. Demonstrate how to set up the lakes. Hold up an example of the labeled coffee filter with the soil in place, and the plastic cup. Explain that it will "rain" through the soil into the "lake" below. Choose a volunteer from the class to help you and explain the procedure for their first "fake lake" test, as follows:

a. Remove the coffee filter containing the soil from the cup, being careful not to spill any soil.

b. Place the cup on a piece of white paper to make it easier to see the color of the water in the cup.

c. Add four drops of Universal Indicator solution directly to the cup (the lake).

d. Have your partner suspend the filter containing the soil over the cup.

e. While your partner holds the filter paper containing the soil over the top of the cup, you secure it around the top of the cup with a rubber band.

f. Measure 20 ml of normal rain (distilled water) in a graduated cylinder and pour it over the soil sample. Announce, "This is the normal rainstorm!" You may have to swirl the water around in the soil sample a little, to make sure it mixes well. **Caution the students NOT to stir the soil-water mixture directly, using a pencil or any other object, as this could easily make a hole in the fragile filter paper, causing the soil to spill into the water below.**

g. When the water drains through the soil and the filter paper into the bottom cup, it will mix with the indicator and change color according to its new acidity. Determine the pH of the lake by matching the color of the solution in the cup with the pH color chart. (Sometimes the color of the soil will interfere with the pH color. This is a real difficulty of soil analysis, which should not be glossed over, but rather pointed out as an example of the difficulties that scientists encounter in trying to obtain accurate results. Encourage your students to do as scientists do, and make the best estimate of the color they can under the circumstances.)

h. Record the pH of the lake after the normal rainstorm, along with the soil type, on the data sheet. (For two samples that show very similar colors, often a side-by-side comparison will point out which is a more acidic pH, and which a more basic one.)

Testing Lake pH

1. Ask for predictions from the class as to what will happen to the pH of the water as it filters through the soil: Will it become more acidic, or more basic? By how much? Will it stay the same? Or might there be different reactions, depending on the type of soil? (You may want to take a poll in the class for their ideas about which of these possibilities is most likely.)

2. Describe to the class the various soil samples that you have available to test. If some of the samples were collected in interesting ways, or from unusual areas, you may want to mention this to the class.

3. Check with the class to make sure they understand the procedure. Emphasize that the four drops of Universal Indicator solution go directly into the cup and remind the class of appropriate safety considerations.

4. Explain that groups of four will share materials, but that pairs of students will work together to test two lakes. Have the class form into groups and distribute one equipment tray to each group. Ask if there are any final questions, then have them begin.

5. Circulate as necessary to make sure the testing is proceeding correctly and respond to questions students may have.

Pooling Data on the Board

1. While the students are busy conducting their tests and recording results, draw a summary table on a large sheet of butcher paper, as in the example on this page. Make sure to leave sufficient space between each soil sample so students will be able to fill in two sets of results, following the steps outlined below.

	0	1	2	3	4	5	6	7	8	9	10	11	12	13	14
GRANITE								XX		XX					
					AAAA										
EUCALYPTUS									XX		XX				
					AAA		A								
PINE				XX		X									
				AAAA											
REDWOOD											XXX		X		
			AA		A										

2. As groups finish, have them record their results on the table on the class chart, by putting an "X" in the appropriate place on the table. Have all groups use a **marker of the same color.**

3. Ask the students to put their equipment aside for the moment and focus their attention on the chart. Ask for suggestions about why different students got different results when testing the same soil type. You may want to point out that scientists have similar difficulties in dealing with variation in results. You may also want to ask students to suggest different ways of analyzing the results, i.e., average? mode? median?

4. With class assistance, rank the lakes in order, from most acidic to least acidic. Or, you may want to take a poll of the class to see how many groups ended up with a lake that had a pH more acidic than water (thumbs up); more basic than water (thumbs down); or no change (arms folded).

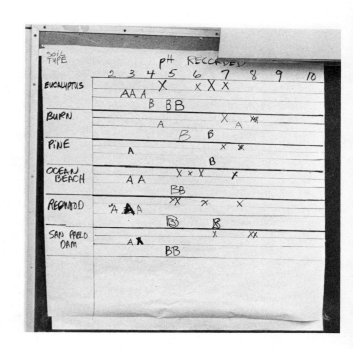

5. Do the results include any examples of "lakes" that are already too acidic for aquatic life to survive comfortably in (regardless of any additional effect by acid rain)? You may also want to ask why some lakes might have a more or less acidic pH than others (for example, those with substrates with a component that has been burned at some stage will usually be quite basic, see "Behind the Scenes," page 123).

Note: Do not extend the discussion of results too much here, unless you have extra time. The main discussion of these results should take place at the beginning of Session 5.

An Acid Rainstorm!

1. Say to the class: "Now suppose a cloud full of pH 3 acid rain comes by and rains on your lake!" Have students predict the probable pH value of their lake after being rained on by acid rain (or take a poll of class predictions, as described above).

2. Explain that, to simulate acid rain, you have made a solution in the laboratory; it has a pH of approximately 3, and contains sulfuric acid, one of the main acids in acid rain. Tell them that they should measure out 20 ml of "acid rain" and pour it through their soil sample. (Students may have to add more indicator to the cup to get a strong enough color to determine the new pH). As before, remind them that a small amount of swirling might be necessary to adequately mix the "acid rain" solution and the soil together in the coffee filter. Also, they should resist stirring with a pencil so they don't accidentally poke a hole in the filter.

3. When each group has finished, they will record the results on the butcher paper chart, on the next line down from their previous results for the same soil, only this time using an "A" (for acid) rather than an "X," and using a **different color marker.**

4. Distribute a bottle of "acid rain" to each group ("Here comes the acid rainstorm!") and have them begin.

Of course, the amount of "acid rain" that students are adding to their "lakes" is much larger proportionally than the amount an acid rainstorm would add to an actual lake. Again, the object here is to graphically demonstrate how substrate and acidity affect lake pH, not to precisely duplicate reality. Interestingly, scientists sometimes use techniques like this, which involve increasing the amount or strength of a particular variable by many times more than usual, in order to obtain intensified results that may allow them to draw inferences about effects at less exaggerated levels.

Reviewing the Data: Effects of Acid Rain

1. Collect the equipment from the groups (or have them deposit it at a convenient location in the room) and select two typical samples of each type of lake, and display them at the front of the class.

2. Re-focus the group's attention. Help them summarize what the main effects of the acid rain were on the lakes with different soil types. Some of the results will be quite predictable, as when the acid rain filters through a soil that does not moderate its pH, so the lake becomes a lot more acidic. Other soils may affect the acid on the way through, and either neutralize, or in some way offset, the effects of the acid rain. What is important to focus on here, at least as much as the final acidity of the lake, is the **amount of change** that the acid rain caused in the acidity of the lake.

3. Now ask students how many of them, after the acid rainstorm, still ended up with a lake with a pH that would support aquatic life of any type. Most groups of students will probably have produced lakes that are now strongly acidified. Interestingly, some soils have natural buffers and can take a large degree of acid precipitation without causing the lakes to become very acidic. The limestone soils and soils from burned areas may still allow the lakes to support life even after this acid rain episode.

4. Defer further discussion of results until the next session, so there is time to introduce the possibility of using buffer to decrease acidity, as outlined below.

Note: If you wish to recycle the plastic cups that had Universal Indicator in them, for use in another class, wash them out as soon as possible after the activity. Otherwise, the cups may be stained.

*High levels of methylmercury are being found in fresh water fish caught in the United States, Canada, and Scandinavia, even in lake waters formerly considered "pristine." Methylmercury is the form of mercury most poisonous to humans and many other animals. At least 21 U.S. states have issued health advisories concerning affected waters. Since many fish are relatively unaffected by low levels of methylmercury, they can accumulate large amounts in their flesh, making eating such fish a serious health hazard. Adults eating large amounts of methylmercury can suffer irreversible nerve damage. Children exposed in utero can develop a range of problems, including psychomotor retardation and severe brain damage. Scientists continue to investigate the complex causes for the apparent increase in methylmercury contamination, including direct industrial pollutants and "fallout" from more distant air polluters. **One of the few features common to waters with this problem is that they all also have a low pH or a steady rain of acidic disposition.** Why fish in such acidic waters may be especially vulnerable to mercury contamination is not known, but the mercury pH link is well documented. For more on methylmercury and its increasing impact on fresh water in many states, see "Mercury's Fishy Fallout" in Science News, the Weekly Newsmagazine of Science, Washington, D.C., Volume 139, Number 10, March 9, 1991.*

Treat Your Lake to a Tums®

1. Hold up a package of Tums. Ask what people usually use Tums tablets for. [Indigestion, acid stomach] Tell the class that Tums is mostly made of a chemical ($CaCO_3$, or calcium carbonate) that acts as a "buffer" in the presence of acid, so it is used as an antacid treatment for stomachs that produce too much acid as a reaction to particular foods, or because of stress. Explain that a *buffer* is a substance that brings an acidified solution, such as a lake, to a less acidic pH. The buffer in Tums changes the pH of an acid stomach to a less acidic, more comfortable one.

2. Explain that the chemical buffer, calcium carbonate, that is in Tums is exactly the same chemical that is actually used to treat acidified lakes in places like Britain and Sweden, and lakes in the Adirondack Mountains in upstate New York. Now you are going to select some of the lakes the students made in class and "treat them to a Tums," to see what happens.

3. Refer to the two lakes of each soil-type showing typical results, that you set at the front of the class when all of the equipment for the experiment was collected. Explain to the class that you are going to treat one of each type of lake with buffer and use the other lake as a control.

4. Take a Tums tablet, and crumble it roughly between your fingers, as you drop it **directly into one of the lakes** (into the cup). Repeat this procedure for one of each type of lake. Leave the other set of lakes untreated, as a control.

5. Tell the class you will set aside these treated and untreated lakes, and observe and record their pH's in the next session (or at least 15–20 minutes later). In the next session, the class will see what happened in the Tums test, and will discuss all the results of the "fake lakes" experiments.

ACID RAIN

WHAT TO DO

1. Remove filter containing soil from cup (don't spill any soil).

2. Place cup on white paper. Add 4 drops of Universal Indicator to cup.

3. Suspend the filter containing the soil across the cup and secure with a rubber band.

4. Measure out 20 ml of normal rain water.

5. Pour the rain water onto the soil, so it drips down into the cup.

6. Record the pH of your lake on the sheet below and on the class chart.

RESULTS

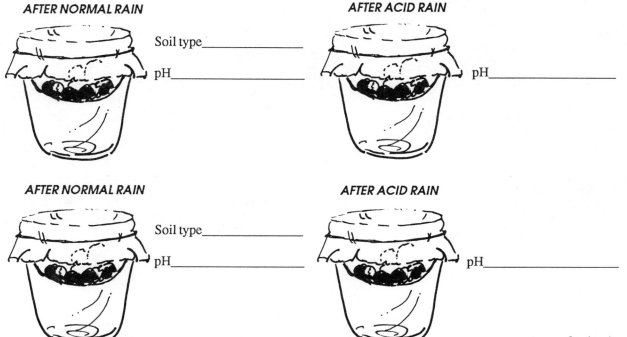

AFTER NORMAL RAIN

Soil type_____

pH_____

AFTER ACID RAIN

pH_____

AFTER NORMAL RAIN

Soil type_____

pH_____

AFTER ACID RAIN

pH_____

Session 5: Welcome to Laketown!

Overview

In this session, the students discuss the effects of the buffer that was added to the acidified "fake lakes" they made in Session 4. After reviewing their experiments, the students draw some conclusions about the success of buffer in returning acidified lakes to a pH that can support aquatic life. The pros and cons of adding buffer to acidified lakes, as a long-range solution to the problem, are considered.

The class then turns its attention to the results of the plant growth experiment set up in Session 1. Students count the number of seeds that were able to germinate in each of the solutions. Class findings are summarized and interpreted.

On the basis of their experimental findings in both the "fake lakes" and plant growth activities, as well as the scientific principles and background information they've covered so far during the unit, the students begin to consider the effects the acid rain problem might have on a lakeside community.

What are the effects of acid rain on the the plants, animals, and people in a community? While it would be difficult and time-consuming to study the complexity of an actual community's response in full scientific and sociological detail, the students can gain insight into these "real-life" problems by preparing, in the second half of this session, and the next, for an "Emergency Town Meeting on Acid Rain," held in Session 7.

The purposes of Session 5 are to: (1) give students practice in analyzing and interpreting the results of experiments that model the effects of human-made chemicals on lake systems; (2) have students analyze and interpret the results of an experiment that investigates the effects of dilute acid on plant growth; and (3) encourage students to begin sorting through the scientific and social components of a real environmental issue, fostering an ability to perceive the problem from a number of different perspectives.

Some classes or individual students may have considerable experience in presenting ideas and viewpoints to groups, while others may have very little. You are best suited to evaluate the experience of your students, so we encourage you to adjust the structure and format of the town meeting as you think best. If you are working in cooperation with other teachers on this unit, or want feedback from others on how to present this section, you could enliven a staff or science department meeting by organizing a run-through of the "Acid Rain Play" (in Session 6) or rehearsing the initial presentations for a simulated town meeting—then your colleagues could share ideas on the best ways to involve various types of students.

While research continues on the effects of acid rain on humans, it is known that the pollutants from which acid rain is made can be harmful. The Director of Environmental and Occupational Medicine at Mount Sinai Hospital in New York has stated that "the pollutants in acid rain are probably third after active smoking and passive smoking as a cause of lung disease." Sulfur dioxide and nitrogen oxide emissions from autos and industry have been linked to increases in the occurrence of asthma and lung disease, especially among children and the elderly. There is a growing body of scientific and medical opinion which suggests that acid rain and acidic particles found in polluted air that people breathe (known as "acid aerosols") may severely damage public health. You and your students may want to research recent magazine and journal articles on this subject. In addition to seeking articles on "acid rain," other key words for research are:"acid aerosol" and "sulfur dioxide." Some references on this subject include: "The Human Cost of Acid Rain" by John R. Luoma and Salvatore Catalano, Audubon magazine, Volume 90, July 1988, page 16. The issue contains several other related articles. Saving the Earth: A Citizen's Guide to Environmental Action by Will Steger and Jon Bowermaster, Alfred A. Knopf, New York, 1990, contains an excellent chapter on acid rain and its effects, pages 71-91.

What You Need

For the class:
- [ ] the table of class results for the "fake lakes" experiment, as recorded on butcher paper in Session 4.
- [ ] the set of demonstration "fake lakes" with the Tums® tablet added, and the set of control "fake lakes," as set up in Session 4.
- [ ] the description of an imaginary town entitled "Welcome to Laketown!" (page 83)
- [ ] 1 copy of each of the 4 group descriptions, for the student groups representing politicians, manufacturers, townspeople, and fisherpeople (masters included, pages 84–85.)

For each group of 4 students:
- [ ] access to the seed germination experiments set up in Session 1.
- [ ] a wooden popsicle stick or toothpick, to assist the students in examining the germination trials.

For each student:
- [ ] 1 copy of the article, "Efforts Continue Against Acid Rain" (master included, page 86)

Getting Ready

Before the Day of the Activity

Duplicate:

- 1 copy of each of the four group descriptions—one for each of the groups.

- 1 copy of the article, "Efforts Continue Against Acid Rain" for each student.

On the Day of the Activity

1. If they are not already posted, put up the results of the "fake lakes" experiments (obtained in Session 4 and recorded on butcher paper) on the classroom wall, in a convenient location, so all students can see them.

2. Set out the demonstration set of "fake lakes" of each soil type that you treated with Tums tablets in Session 4, along with the control set of lakes of each soil type subjected to acid rain, but without any Tums treatment.

3. Have available for examination the seed germination trials that the class set up in Session 1.

Reviewing the "Fake Lakes" and Buffer Results

1. Refer the class to the posted table of experimental results from Session 4. Ask the students, "What do you think were the most important results of the experiment?" If responses do not include the following, ask: "What happened to the pH of each of the lake types after normal rain?" "What happened to the pH in each case after the acid rainstorm?"

2. Ask the class to recall what range of pH will safely support aquatic life. [pH 5–9] Ask if any of their lakes were still able to support life after the acid rainstorm. If some were, ask them what might account for this. [Some soil substrates have natural buffers or bases that can neutralize or partially offset the effects of acid solution flowing through them.]

3. Explain that what the class observed in their model lakes (that some lakes were less acidic than others after an acid rain, depending on the reaction of the substrate to the acid) is what scientists call a lake's *buffering capacity.* Each type of lake substrate has a certain buffering capacity, or ability to make the lake less acidic. Some lakes can neutralize a lot of acid before becoming acidic themselves, while other lakes have little or no buffering capacity.

4. Focus attention on the two demonstration sets of "fake lakes" from the previous session. Remind the class that one set was treated with a buffer (half of a crushed Tums tablet) after being "rained on" by acid rain, and the other is a control set subjected to acid rain but not treated with the buffer. Adding buffer is an artificial way of attempting to increase a lake's buffering capacity.

5. Ask for two volunteers to determine the pH of each buffer-treated lake, and have them record the pH for each of these lakes on the class results table, in each case underneath the previously recorded pH values for the original lake water, and the lake water as affected by acid rain. You might want to record these new results with a different color marker.

6. Ask the class if any of the buffer-treated lakes would now have a pH better able to support aquatic life than their control lakes. Ask them to indicate which of the lakes did not recover pH sufficiently to support aquatic life.

Note: Only a few soil substrates will produce lakes that are not able to be treated successfully with a buffer, in particular, red-colored iron-rich soils. This may be due to the calcium carbonate buffer being used up in a reaction with the iron in the soil.

7. Many of the lakes should now be "healthy" again. In discussion, help the class sum up the effect of the buffer solution on the acidity of the lakes. [In most cases, the buffer should bring the pH toward some median point, approaching, although not necessarily reaching, pH 7.]

8. Remind the class that the active ingredient of Tums is calcium carbonate and that calcium carbonate is the same chemical that has been used to treat small acidified lakes in some countries. It is also the chemical in some natural lake substrates that allows such lakes to have a large buffering capacity and therefore be protected from acid rain. In fact, treating lakes with large quantities of

buffer is one of the solutions now in effect for small-sized acid lakes in Canada, Britain, Scandinavia, and some parts of the United States. Airplanes and trucks dump huge loads of naturally-occurring calcium carbonate into lakes or onto the surrounding soil. Calcium carbonate is found in limestone or chalk deposits and mined in large quantities.

9. You may also want to point out that buffer is used in home aquariums and swimming pools to control the pH. Some students may have had experience with these.

10. Ask your class if they can think of any problems with adding buffer to a lake. [It is a sudden, intrusive change to the ecosystem—the presence of large amounts of buffer chemicals can be disastrous to some organisms, directly harming some and disrupting the lifecycles of others. While treatment with buffer might be a reasonable first step in some cases, it is less likely to be effective for continuing long-term acidification problems. The cost is quite high—buffer treatment has been estimated at $50,000 per year for a small lake and the process may have to be repeated annually.]

11. Help the class summarize the results of the "fake lake" experiment by asking the following questions: What contributes to the pH of lake water? Why does acid rain affect the pH of some lakes differently than other lakes? What are the advantages and disadvantages of treating acidified lakes with buffers like calcium carbonate?

12. If the following points do not come up in your students' discussion, be sure to bring them up yourself:

   a. In the natural environment, some lakes (and streams) are naturally more acidic than others, due to the soil surrounding the lake and the chemicals in the water.

   b. In these lakes, the aquatic life is more adapted to acidic conditions; they can live comfortably at lower pH's than organisms in other lakes.

If you or some of your students have aquariums, you might want to test the water for its pH, and also test the effects of buffer on the aquarium water. An interesting point in this connection is that water in aquariums is usually treated with buffer to keep it from becoming too **basic.** *See "Behind the Scenes" on page 123, for more information on how buffers are used to alter the pH of both acids and bases. The GEMS guide, Mapping Fish Habitats, describes a series of classroom aquarium experiments that students can conduct to investigate fish habitats.*

The article in New Scientist *(see "Resources" section for reference listing) contains much information on several buffering approaches. After discussing the pros and cons of treating lakes with calcium carbonate, and detailing the newer method of "catchment liming," which applies calcium carbonate to the catchment, or land around lakes and rivers, the New Scientist article concludes, "However much catchment liming may benefit fish, it almost inevitably causes ecological damage . . . although liming can help a single species, it is not appropriate for conserving whole habitats. In the end, liming only treats the symptoms—the cure is to reduce the emissions of acids at the source."*

· SEED GERMINATION RATE ·

	SUNFLOWER	PEA
100% VINEGAR		
20% VINEGAR		
10% VINEGAR		
5% VINEGAR		
1% VINEGAR		
WATER		

You may want to assist your students in converting the germination scores (out of 10 seeds) into percentages by showing that simply multiplying by 10 yields the percentage, for example, by noting that 2 out of 10 = 20%, 5 out of 10 = 50% and so on.

c. Some substrates that surround lakes are more effective than others in neutralizing the effects of acid rain.

13. Point out that the students' models demonstrate that the effects of acid rain are much more complex than rain simply coming down into a lake and changing the pH of that lake. In fact, there is a *system* of interacting components, including the rain, the soil (or lake substrate), and the lake water. Modeling experiments, such as those the class conducted, are used by scientists to try to predict what effects acid rain may have on different acid lakes and streams. Ask your students what limitations their "fake lakes" might have, as models of how lakes are affected by acid rain.

Healthy Plants or Pickled Beansprouts Revisited

1. Summarize by saying that the class has just analyzed the results of an experiment that models the effects of acid rain on a lake's acidity. Lake acidity has important consequences for the life in and around a lake. Now it's time to take a look at this aspect in more depth, by analyzing the results of the seed germination experiment they began in the first session.

2. Students will count the number of seeds germinated in each of their trials (water and various strengths of vinegar) and write these results in the appropriate place on the board. They should record their results as a percent. For example, if two out of their ten seeds germinated, they should record 20%. Organize the class into the same groups that set up the germination trials in Session 1. Ask them if they have any questions, have them collect their own experiments, and begin.

3. As the students observe and count, draw a data chart on the board, as in the example on this page.

4. Ask the class what they think about the results. There will probably be a clear difference in the germination rates in water and full strength vinegar, with the germination rates for dilutions of vinegar being somewhere in between. (Sometimes, the germination rate in some dilutions of vinegar may be as low as the full strength vinegar rates, or as high as the water germination rates, depending on the sensitivity of that particular seed type to acid.)

5. You may want to further discuss the differences in germination rates, as they relate to the different types of seed used. Point out that scientific research has found similar results. Ask the class what they think their results suggest about the effects of acid rain on living organisms in lakes. Point out that some plants and animals are more sensitive than others to pH levels, and at different stages in their life cycles. This is because organisms have a complex series of chemical reactions going on in their bodies at any given time, and these reactions need to occur at specific pH's. If the pH is changed, the chemical reactions that lead to germination, growth, reproduction, or other life processes, may be abnormally affected.

For example, Eastern Tiger Salamander adults can live in a low pH. Their eggs are surrounded by a jelly-like substance that normally protects the egg. However, in acidified lakes, this jelly absorbs the acid and stops development of the salamander young. Studies have found that a pH of 5.5 is acidic enough to kill half of the eggs, and, at a pH below 5, more than two-thirds of the eggs die.

Planning For The Town Meeting

Introduce the Town Meeting

1. Inform the class that in the session after next, they are going to represent the viewpoints of different interest groups at an Emergency Town Meeting called to discuss the acid rain problem affecting an imaginary town named Laketown. For most of the rest of this session, they are going to begin planning what they want to say on behalf of their interest groups at the town meeting. Tell them that the main purposes of the town meeting will be to clarify the problems affecting the town and to consider possible solutions.

2. Explain that four main groups will be represented at the town meeting: Manufacturers, Fishing People, Politicians, Local Residents. List these on the board. Tell the class that you would like them to be thinking about which one of the four groups they would like to be in as you tell them more about Laketown. Read out loud the description of the town entitled "Welcome to Laketown!" (page 83)

Organize the Interest Groups

1. Remind the class that there are four different groups represented at the town meeting, and they need to decide which one they'd like to be in. Point out that everyone may not get their first choice, because the numbers should be relatively equal, but you will do your best to respond to their selections.

2. Read the names of the four groups out loud. If you think your students need more information before choosing, you may want to read the group descriptions, located at the end of this session (pages 84, 85).

3. Ask for volunteers for each group. Based on your overall judgment and experience with the class, set up the four working groups.

4. Inform the four groups that they will have some time to prepare for the town meeting now and in the next session. For the rest of this session, they will need to appoint people to the following jobs:

> a. a **Reader,** who will read out loud the starting information given to the group by the teacher.
>
> b. a **Writer,** who will note down what the group discusses and decides, and what it wants to say at the town meeting.
>
> c. two **Presenters,** who, on behalf of the group, will present the case to the town meeting.
>
> d. one or more **Clarifiers,** to listen carefully to the ideas suggested, and try to put them into words that can be easily understood and written down.
>
> (Write shortened versions of these on the board.)

5. Then the groups should:

    a. **Read through the group description** together, to make sure everyone in the group understands the situation of their group.

    b. **Discuss what point of view** they are going to present as a group.

    c. **Jot down any questions** they have, either to be asked of other groups, or of the teacher, such as additional background information about their group or the town.

6. Emphasize that when this planning session ends, you will be collecting all the notes on the group's position and any questions generated by the group and recorded by the Writer. These will be returned with your comments at the start of the next planning session.

7. Distribute the four interest group descriptions, and let the groups begin their planning, following the above instructions. Circulate to make sure the groups have appointed people to the various tasks and are proceeding. You will probably need to make up responses to group questions about the specific conditions in the town. Be imaginative and creative, but at the same time be consistent and make sure groups keep to the central issues.

8. With five minutes left at the end of the session, bring group discussions to a close. Collect their notes and any questions they've written down (which can be used to help evaluate and plan the issues and directions of the next phase of planning for the Town Meeting, in Session 6) and bring the class back together.

Homework Reading: Solutions to Acid Rain

1. Hand out the homework reading assignment: "Efforts Continue Against Acid Rain." Explain that it is a compilation of some of the latest information about acid rain, in the form of a newspaper article.

2. Have your students read the article before the next session, reminding them the information in it should be very useful in planning their case at the town meeting.

3. Also as part of the homework, ask the class to list possible solutions from the article, or that they have thought of themselves, for discussion during the next session.

WELCOME TO LAKETOWN!

"Laketown" is a small city of about 75,000 people, on the shore of Lake Imagination, a large lake near the Misty Mountains. Laketown was first settled over 200 years ago, as a fishing village. It was the hometown of several heroes of the 1776 Revolutionary War, and their small cottages are now historic monuments. In the 1800s, Laketown became an important stop for railroad traffic. It is a very scenic and beautiful city, but lately serious problems have surfaced.

•

Fishing is still an important industry, but less so in recent years because it has become harder to catch fish in large quantities, and there are new limits on numbers of fish that can be caught. Many local residents still fish for sport. Lake Imagination has also become a popular resort and vacation spot, so many of the commercial fishing boats are starting to be used for tourist fishing, or to take hikers and campers to islands and forest areas around the lake. Tourism has partly helped ease the high unemployment in the town, but there are still many people without jobs.

Recently several major new industries started operation in industrial parks on the outskirts of town. These companies came because the land is relatively cheap, the railway is close by, and electricity costs from the coal-powered plant in the next valley are low. One of the most exciting new industries is a large plant that produces blank audiotape cassettes, records, and C.D. disks. This involves high-energy processes, such as heating and shaping plastics and metals. The company, Planetary Audio, has put in pollution control equipment that meets the existing environmental standards. But some people say that these controls are not strict enough. They believe the new industries, and emissions from the electric plant that supplies them with energy, cause too much air pollution.

The townspeople are very upset about pollution. Many of them moved to Laketown to get away from the big cities. Some residents are aware of the way that emissions from factories and electric power plants contribute to acid rain. Fumes from the factories that use plastics and metal, and even from the power plant, often sweep through town when the wind blows from their direction. All the historic statues and monuments in town show serious erosion, and the lake water has become much more acidic. Some fishing people blame this acidity for the low catches in recent years. The drinking water is getting more salty and chlorinated, and some parts of the lake are sealed off as unsuitable for swimming. Also, sections of the lush forest that dot the lakeshore have begun to go brown and die.

If the manufacturers are successful in Laketown, they have plans to expand their operations. Some politicians support this, as it would bring more jobs. Others argue that the changes to the environment caused by pollution are destroying the town's natural beauty and will doom the growing tourist industry. All agree that Laketown is facing serious problems and that unless something is done immediately, their once beautiful lakeside community could find its health and vitality threatened and even destroyed. That's why the citizens of Laketown have decided to hold an "Emergency Town Meeting" on acid rain and related matters, to see if, through analysis and discussion, they can come up with some possible solutions to the environmental crisis they face.

Manufacturers

Some of you have owned factories in or near Laketown for many years; others arrived more recently. You make lots of goods for the town and state, and provide townspeople with many jobs. First you were told that the smoke from your factories caused acid rain. You began to clean up the smoke, but in the middle of this were required by new, stricter laws to clean it up even more. The newer manufacturers in your group, such as Planetary Audio, have pollution controls that meet the current standards, but they too have been criticized. Some of the local residents and fishing people say that manufacturers need to stop polluting altogether, no matter what it takes. You are very worried about this, because it's expensive to add new pollution controls. That means that the costs of your products go up, and profits for you and the people who invest in your factories go down. If the laws are too strict, you think you might have to close some factories, and lay workers off. Some of the more recently arrived companies may get discouraged by more controls and move away, which would be a big loss to the local economy.

•

Fishing People

You are a mixed group, including: professionals, who supply the local restaurants and stores with fresh fish; fishing guides, who own boats that take tourists on fishing trips; and members of the local fishing club. You all have one thing in common that is of great concern: over the past 15 years there has been a noticeable decrease in the number of fish in Lake Imagination. One species of fish, the "Imagination Trout," once a popular item in local restaurants, seems to have died out altogether. Although the government has put strict controls on the number and size of fish that can be taken from the lake, the problem seems to be getting worse. All of the evidence seems to point to acid rain as the cause. You are worried that, if something isn't done soon, there won't be any fish left at all. That will mean the end of the fishing industry, the fishing club, and most of the tourist trade as well, bringing unemployment for many of you. One of the most beautiful natural wonders in the region, Lake Imagination, will become a "dead lake," and that would be a tragedy.

•

Politicians

You were elected by citizens who often express their concern about the environment. You promised progress in cleaning up acid pollution in the Laketown area, but the problem has not been solved, even by stricter pollution laws. There is growing discussion in the town about how to protect Lake Imagination and who has a right to use it. You want to find a solution that is acceptable to everyone, but that seems very difficult. You would like to support stricter pollution control laws, but some of the manufacturers are threatening to close down their factories if stricter controls are passed. But you also know that if something isn't done soon, the fishing guides will be unemployed and the local environment could be ruined. Almost every solution seems to call for lots of money, which means asking people to pay more taxes, hardly a popular position, but perhaps a necessary one. Besides this, your experience is that money, by itself, doesn't necessarily solve this sort of problem. Nonetheless, this issue is fast becoming a major crisis, and as an elected representative, you are being urged by more and more groups and individuals to "do something."

•

Local Residents

Some of you have lived near the lake for many years, even generations; others moved to Laketown because of the beautiful environment, thinking that you could get away from the problems of the big city. Now you find that some of the trees and bushes in the forest near the lake are dying, along with the fish in the lake. In addition, the old stone buildings and statues in town are rapidly eroding, and the water supply, which comes from the lake, is getting worse and tastes of chlorine. As citizens and taxpayers you are increasingly concerned that your elected representatives are not doing enough about the problem. Although you are concerned about possible loss of jobs, you are convinced that new and stronger steps must be taken. You want your children and grandchildren to be able to enjoy the wonders and beauties that the Laketown environment offers, and you feel a special responsibility to preserve it for them. Some residents are more concerned about acid rain than others, but more and more believe that if something isn't done soon, it will be too late.

•

EFFORTS

CONTINUE AGAINST
ACID RAIN

■■■■■■■■■■■■■■■■■■■■■■■■■■■■■■■■■

Conference Sets Research Goal ≈≈ *Solutions Remain Elusive*

(Washington) Scientists and environmentalists, meeting today in the nation's capital to discuss solutions to the acid rain crisis, agreed on only one thing—until more is known about all the effects of acid rain, a total solution to the problem remains elusive. The conference, which also included representatives from other countries and from industry, was co-sponsored by the Environmental Protection Agency (EPA) and a citizen's group known as START (for Stop Acid Rain Today).

In its final session, the conference approved a resolution calling for a major increase in funding for acid rain research. Current research results on the effects of acid rain are hotly debated. One recent study on trees indicates that acid rain has a directly harmful effect only on the red spruce, and that there is no proven evidence that acid rain harms other mountain trees. Environmentalists have countered that one-quarter of all trees at higher elevations are red spruce, and that, until further research is done, it would be wrong to assume that acid rain does not harm other trees. Such research, all agree, is complicated by the difficulty of separating out the harmful effects of acid rain from the damage other pollution, heat, drought, cold, and insects inflict on trees.

The effects of acid rain on lakes and streams, on the other hand, are well-known and deadly. Chemicals called buffers (similar to stomach antacid tablets) have been used to neutralize the acid in lakes. However, a Norwegian scientist attending the conference explained that experiments in Norway have shown that this method is only practical for small lakes and streams. Other attendees at the Acid Rain Action conference noted that as long as acid rain water keeps entering a lake, buffer has to be added, and that large amounts of buffer are not only expensive, but could also have unforeseen negative consequences on aquatic life.

The Clean Air Acts of 1970 and 1977 were aimed at reducing the emission of sulfur and nitrogen oxides that produce acid rain. Most attendees agreed that there has been some reduction in the pollution that leads to acid rain, but the laws still leave standards up to individual states. If a state with strict standards adjoins one with less strict controls, the first state often suffers when emissions from the second state drift over it. Environmentalists have criticized industries who claim to be solving the acid rain problem in their local area by building higher smokestacks. Studies show such smokestacks only succeed in distributing the acid rain pollutants (oxides of sulfur and nitrogen) over a wider area.

Technological methods to reduce the sulfur oxides in industrial emissions remain in the experimental stage. There are ways to remove the sulfur from coal, gasoline, and diesel fuels prior to burning, during burning, or in the smokestack after burning, but so far any largescale attempt to implement these methods is seen as impractical because they would probably use more energy and be too expensive.

A spokesperson for START called on the general population to be more aware of the role that their own lifestyles play in acid rain-related pollution, for example excessive use of household heating and private cars. She urged people to consider car-pooling and better housing insulation. She said that a longterm solution to the problem depends on less use of oil, gas, and coal fuels, and much more use of alternative energy sources, especially solar energy.

Conference organizers said they plan to lobby Congress to fund a major research study. They also announced that another Acid Rain Action conference will be held in New York City next year. Despite the lack of agreement on solutions, activists believe that focusing attention on the problem is a good first step in itself.

Session 6: The Salamanders Have Their Say

Overview

This session begins with a discussion of the homework assignment, focusing on possible solutions to the problems posed by acid rain. The discussion helps orient the students toward considering additional solutions during their town meeting preparation in the latter part of the session.

Before further preparation for the meeting begins, however, it is time for the salamanders and other lake organisms to "have their say" via "Acid Rain—The Play," a short, scripted dramatization that transports the students' imaginations into a lake ecosystem affected by acid rain. In the play, aquatic animals and plants discuss what is happening to them and what they might do about it. The class discusses biological concepts arising out of the play that are helpful in understanding the possible effects of acid rain. The play also serves as a vehicle for discussing the range of different points of view and reactions that people may have to complex environmental/social problems such as acid rain (modeled by the stereotyped reactions of the characters in the play). This discussion serves as a bridge to the continuing preparations for the town meeting, as students meet in their interest groups to creatively consider some of the possible alternatives and solutions that might be acceptable to other interests represented at the meeting.

The purposes of the session are to: (1) provide additional information, and promote discussion, about possible solutions to problems caused by acid rain; (2) convey some of the ways that acid rain affects biological systems, in a dramatic, interesting, and informative way; (3) highlight some of the stereotyped ways in which people sometimes react to difficult environmental and community issues, and encourage the students to think more in terms of alternative, creative solutions to these problems, stressing conciliation rather than conflict; and (4) provide students with additional discussion time, resources, and organizational direction, in preparing their presentations for the simulated town meeting in the next session.

What You Need

For the class:
- ☐ 7 large index cards or half sheets of paper
- ☐ 1 large sheet of butcher paper
- ☐ 1 marker
- ☐ masking tape
- ☐ 8 copies of the script of "Acid Rain: The Play" (master included, pages 100–103).
- ☐ 4 "Possible Solutions" sheets, 1 each for the politicians, manufacturers, townspeople, fisherpeople (masters included, pages 104–105)

Getting Ready

Before the Day of the Activity

1. **Make large name signs** for each character in the play. Because there are a number of characters in the play, the audience can find it difficult to remember which character is speaking without some indication. Use a marker to write the following names and descriptors on the large cards (you may even want to include simple drawings or cartoons of each of the characters on these cards, or have some artistically-inclined students help you):

Phyto the Plant
(searching for a solution)

Flitters the Insect
(can't make up its mind)

Truttie the Brown Trout
(the pessimist)

Perch the Perch
(the postponer)

Sal the Salamander—lives at the south end of the lake
(worried—desperate to find a solution)

Mander the Salamander—lives at the north end of the lake
(a simple optimist)

Rocky the Raccoon
(a touch of wisdom)

Some teachers have found the name signs easier to read if they are mounted on a stick, so the actors can hold them up. Others have used string so the actors can wear the signs around their necks. Many teachers find it useful to further dramatize the play, either by providing players with simple costumes (plain paper bags with various character-faces drawn on them serve as simple paper masks) or by getting the class to produce these themselves.

A number of teachers have also found it useful to have the selected actors read through the play once before presenting it, or even rehearse it more fully. One way to do this is to set aside extra time in a previous class period, for the eight selected students to read over/rehearse their parts in the play separately, while the other students work in groups to make costumes or background scenery. Paying this sort of attention to dramatic preparation is likely to be more popular with younger groups, but mostly depends on the reaction of your class to the idea. Preparations for the play could also be combined with drama or art classes at your school to more fully explore the interdisciplinary enrichment of this unit.

2. **Duplicate:**

- Eight copies of the script of "Acid Rain: The Play" — one for each of the lake characters, and one for the teacher.

- One copy of each of the four sample solution sheets —one for each of the groups.

3. Read through the notes and questions turned in by the interest groups at the end of the previous session. Make written comments in response to these questions and suggestions, and note other ideas and issues each group might consider. These will be returned to the interest groups in the second part of Session 6, for their consideration during the final preparation of their presentations for the town meeting in Session 7.

 Generating Solutions

Discussing the Homework

1. Ask the class for their thoughts about the homework article they read.

2. Based on the article, and their experiments, and whatever other information they've gained, have them raise their hands and each state one possible solution to the acid rain problem. Be sure to tell the students that partial solutions, or things that might help, rather than completely solve, the problem, are definitely worth raising. Encourage them to be creative and inventive.

3. As the students make their suggestions, summarize and list them on a large sheet of butcher paper.

4. Remind the class that among the major sources of the oxides of sulfur and nitrogen are coal-burning power plants and cars. You may want to ask them to summarize how acid rain is formed, and then ask if there are any additional suggestions to add to the proposed solutions list.

5. Suggest to the class that the list of solutions you have generated together should be referred to as they work in their interest groups (later in the session) in preparation for the town meeting.

We recommend that you do not provide students with a list of possible solutions at this stage—it is far better for them to come up with their own. However, you should be aware, and may want to allude in subsequent discussions, to one or more of the following solutions that have been proposed for the acid rain problem:

taller smoke stacks
buffers in lakes
breeding acid-resistant fish
many energy conservation measures
 (such as mass transit alternatives to
 private cars, improved housing
 insulation, recycling containers and
 packaging that take lots of energy and
 materials to produce)
desulfurization and denitrification of fuels
 or smokestack gases
increased use of fuels naturally low
 in sulfur
creation of new technologies to reduce
 emissions
substitution of fossil fuels by other energy
 alternatives

Why Solutions Are Needed

1. Tell the class that the solutions they have generated are good first steps. Point out that although the problem of acid rain is serious, there is great potential for finding solutions.

2. Ask them to recall the serious consequences of acid rain.

3. Explain that many of these problems can be solved if we, as citizens of this planet, take charge and address the problems with solutions like the class has generated with this list. Point out that workable, practical solutions often take a lot of effort, and that sometimes people seem to need to personally witness or identify with the damage before deciding it is worth the effort to solve the problem.

4. Tell the class they are about to present a dramatic reading of a play, depicting aquatic animals and a plant who have assembled to discuss and solve the problem of acid rain. It is fitting that the characters are aquatic animals, because they are among the first to feel the adverse effects of acid rain.

Acid Rain — The Play

Introduce the Play

1. Tell the class that the purpose of the model lakes in Session 4 was to provide an idea of what the buffering capacity of a lake is. Point out that the model was limited because lakes are living *ecosystems*—the model was not able to show the effects of acid rain on the plants and animals living in the lakes (i.e., it was a physical model, not a biological model). One way of getting to know the biological part of a lake is to do field tests on it, but that is not possible in the time available for this unit. (See "Going Further" page 120 for some ideas on extending the unit in this way.)

2. Tell the class that it is possible, however, to visit a lake today, for a little while, to see what is going on there. Say, "you can visit a lake by using your imagination, and the vehicle to transport you there will be a play, entitled "Acid Rain: The Play."

Set Up the Play

1. Explain that some members of the class will present a dramatic reading of a play about what might happen to the organisms in a lake threatened by acid rain. The rest of the class is the audience for the play. Encourage everyone to take careful note of the issues raised by the play—both what happens to an acidified lake, and how different characters react to the problems.

2. Tell the class there are seven characters in the play and you are going to briefly describe each of them, then ask for a volunteer. Read out the first character description. (See the character descriptions on page 99. You may want to just list the characters with a very brief description or read the longer characterizations provided. Other creative alternatives for presenting the play are suggested in "Getting Ready" for this session.)

3. Assign a student to play each character. Give them a sign to hold or hang around their neck (that tells the audience which character they are) and a script. (When you assign characters, consider which student will represent the character well, without disrupting the flow of the play. Depending on your judgment, students with reading difficulties can either be encouraged by assigning them a minor part, or not chosen, for the sake of the flow, and to avoid embarrassment.)

4. Set up a "fishbowl." Have each of the characters assemble in an open space toward the front of the room, and ask the other students to sit in a larger semi-circle, spread out in front of the players, and close enough so everyone is able to hear even the more soft-spoken actors. Encourage the actors to perform dramatically, to talk slowly, and to project clearly.

Read & Discuss the Play

1. Introduce the play by reading the setting out loud (labelled "Narrator/ Teacher" at the beginning of the script). Have the players read through the play without comment, either from yourself or from the watching students.

2. At the end of the play, with students still sitting in the same positions, ask the class what they learned about what happens to an ecosystem in and near a lake that is subjected to acid rain. You might start by asking, "Who are the 'Two-Legs?'" In the discussion, help bring out the following points:

> • It is not only the lake water that is affected by acid rain. The organisms that live in the water can be affected, which in turn affects other organisms in the ecosystem of the lake.

> • Plants are at the base of the food chain, so if acid rain affects them, it affects everything.

> • Some organisms are more affected by low pH than others. Different organisms are affected in different ways.

> • Different parts of a lake can be affected in different ways.

> • Some organisms might seem to benefit by acid rain in the short term, as, for example, if other species they compete with for food decrease or die out. However, in the long-term the reduced diversity of organisms means that the lake will have less of a chance of surviving severe environmental stress, such as droughts, nutrient loads, or other poisons dumped into the lake, because these other species might have been the key to the lake ecosystem being able to surmount these severe stresses.

Some students may falsely conclude that if acid contaminates a plant, it will in turn contaminate an animal that eats that plant, and so on up the food chain. While this is how some poisons, heavy metals, and radioactive substances can "get into the food chain," it is not the case with acid rain. When acid affects a plant, it may cause the plant to die, thus affecting the next link in the food chain by eliminating that plant as a source of food. If enough plants die, the survival of the animals that eat such plants is threatened, and this could have a domino-like effect on the entire food chain.

● Buffers can be used to treat some acid-affected lakes in the short term, but in the long term this is too costly, or is damaging to the ecosystem in other ways. You may want to conduct a very brief discussion on the limitations of buffer as a long-term solution. (See "Behind the Scenes," page 123 for additional discussion of buffers.)

3. Ask the class what different points of view were represented in the play:

● Did the different characters have different perspectives on the problem?

● Did the students recognize any typical responses that *people* might have to environmental/community problems, as represented by the different lake characters?

● Can anyone give an example of a situation where they've heard people talking in similar ways?

● Were all the different perspectives useful? Which ones do they think were useful, and which ones weren't? Why?

4. Emphasize that different people also react to the acid rain problem in different ways, just as the characters did in the play. In fact, this is one of the main challenges people face: how to sort out, from all the different points of view, what the best things to do about a problem are (provided we all agree that the problem exists). Being able to discuss and decide on solutions that work and that take into account differing priorities and viewpoints can be a difficult task, but it is a very necessary and rewarding one. It can help promote increased group understanding and a better sense of community.

5. Explain that one of the main purposes of the town meeting is to look for creative solutions to the problems confronting the town. In presenting their cases to the town meeting, and suggesting alternatives, the interest groups should not see themselves as belonging to different teams that are in competition with one another, and should not engage in a debate that each of the groups is trying to win. At the same time, the differences and dilemmas faced by each of the groups cannot be ignored or smoothed over, and have to be dealt with directly. Suggest that the students don't act like the less constructive characters in the play, but rather try to clearly understand the interests they are representing and pose solutions that represent those interests and, at the same time, might be acceptable to other groups as well.

Final Planning for the Town Meeting

Organize the Interest Groups

1. Explain to the class that in a few minutes, they will be getting back together in their town meeting interest groups. Remind them of the jobs they were assigned in the last session: reader, writer, presenters, and clarifier(s). You may want to list these on the board.

2. Remind the groups that they have three main tasks in preparing for the town meeting:

   a. A **description of** their group's **main points of view** about the town's problems with acid rain.

   b. A **list of questions or comments** they want to pose to other groups at the town meeting.

   c. Some ideas about **possible solutions** to the acid rain problem that are acceptable to more than one interest group at the town meeting.

   (Summarize each of these tasks on the board).

In some classes, the teacher has encouraged each group to send a representative to other groups, both to lobby on behalf of its proposals, and to find out what the other groups are proposing. Of course, the nature and extent of this sort of interchange will depend in large part on the experience and maturity of the class. Those classes that have difficulty staying organized and accomplishing the main tasks definitely do not need this additional complication. On the other hand, classes that are more sophisticated can enliven the meeting and make proposed solutions more realistic and complex by lobbying and negotiating.

As one alternative to having representatives from one group lobby or negotiate with another, you may want to help sort out solutions that seem most widely acceptable as you circulate from group to group. For example, you could take a solution that arises in one group to another group and discuss possible responses with them, then continue this process with several other proposed solutions.

3. Tell the groups that when they are ready to begin work, you will return their questions from the previous planning session to them, along with your comments and suggestions, and you will hand out "Possible Solution" sheets. Emphasize that the solutions are meant only as examples of the types of things that the group might suggest to the town meeting. Encourage the students to make up their own, more relevant or more widely acceptable solutions.

4. Tell the class that you will again collect their notes at the end of this session to go over them before the meeting.

5. Ask if there are any questions, then have them begin.

Finalize the Town Meeting Presentations

1. During the small group discussions, circulate among the groups to offer suggestions and clarify what the circumstances of the group are. If a group is short on ideas, direct them to the description of their group, and the suggested solutions that you have handed out.

Note: You will probably be called on to use your own imagination and judgment in helping the groups develop ideas to present at the town meeting. Some teachers have allowed groups to send representatives to lobby other groups regarding the acceptability of some of their solutions. Also refer back to the description of the town ("Welcome to Laketown!") and feel free to expand on it. Students may also have suggestions about other circumstances in the town, and you can use these to enhance and enliven the discussion about the town's dilemma and possible solutions to the acid rain problem. Students may also want to enhance specifics regarding their groups or subgroups, for example by naming the fishing club, detailing specific companies and what they manufacture, and so on.

2. Five minutes before the end of the session, remind students that they should have a clear written statement about who the group is, how they view the problem of acid rain in relation to the town, and what solutions they would like to propose.

3. At the end of the session, collect each of the groups' preparation notes. You will probably want to look these over, in preparing for your task as Mayor at the town meeting in the next session, and especially in relation to finding possible solutions that are broadly acceptable.

4. Before the class ends, mention that they will have five minutes at the beginning of the next session (before the town meeting begins) to go over what they have written and make any final changes. Encourage the students to keep thinking about additional points they might want to make at the town meeting, and new solutions that might be acceptable to some or all of the other interest groups.

Fishbowl
ACID RAIN: *The Play*

•

THE CAST OF CHARACTERS

1. **Phyto** the Aquatic Plant—lives underwater at the edge of the lake.

2. **Flitters** the Swimming Insect—lives in the water, near the shore.

3. **Truttie** the Brown Trout—lives near the surface of the water.

4. **Perch** the Perch—lives on the bottom of the lake.

5. **Sal** the Salamander—lives at the south end of the lake.

6. **Mander** the Salamander—lives at the north end of the lake.

7. **Rocky** the Raccoon—lives in the forest at the edge of the lake.

CHARACTERIZATIONS

1. **Phyto the Plant:** The baseline of the ecosystem—the one who is trying to find a solution, and trying to deal with the other personalities.

> *"You shouldn't be so hard on X and Y; I think they have a good point when they say . . . "*

2. **Flitters the Insect:** Flitters about from one opinion to the other—can't make up its mind, always bending with the argument, trying to find an easy solution.

> *"Yes, well now I think X is right. We shouldn't be worried at all . . . but on the other hand . . . "*

3. **Truttie the Brown Trout:** Worried and panicky, with good reason—cannot survive below pH 6—always the pessimist, always looking at the most bleak future.

> *"Look, unless we do something now, we'll all be doomed . . . "*

4. **Perch the Perch:** The postponer, happy to deal with things later rather than sooner, able to withstand pH down to 4.5—not inclined to change mind easily.

> *"Let's not jump to hasty conclusions—we're not even sure this is being caused by acid rain . . . "*

5. **Sal the Salamander:** Lives at the south end of the lake, where the acidity has been worst—trying to work out what to do about it, getting very worried.

> *"I just can't understand how this whole thing has suddenly started happening . . . "*

6. **Mander the Salamander:** Lives at the north end of the lake, where changes haven't started yet—a simple optimist who doesn't really want to know what is going on.

> *"I think it will all work out just fine—it always has in the past . . . "*

7. **Rocky the Raccoon:** Lives by the edge of the lake; eats things from the forest and people's garbage cans as well as fish—measured and wise, able to introduce new perspectives (e.g., human).

> *"That may be true, X, but these changes are also going on in the forest nearby."*

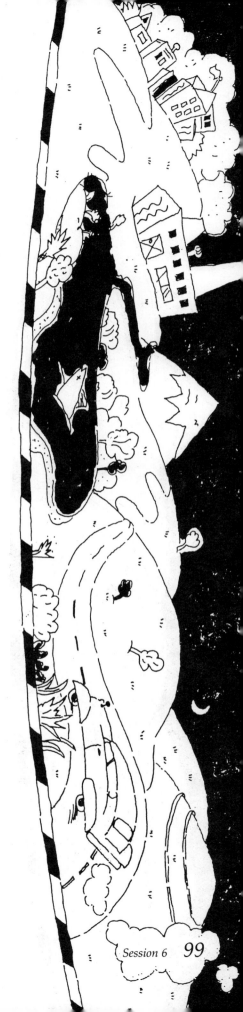

ACID RAIN: *The Play*

Narrator/Teacher: The scene is a rock at the edge of a large lake in the northeastern United States. Some of the animals and plants that live in the lake are gathering at the rock, to talk about what is happening to their lake. Of course, such a meeting could never happen in real life, but if it did, it might sound something like this:

•

Perch: So what's up Phyto?

Sal: Yeah, how come you called us all together?

Phyto: I called you here because I am so worried, I can barely photosynthesize. Look, you guys all need us plants to survive, am I right?

Everyone: Yeah!

Mander: Yeah, but did we have to meet out here during the day? Man, it is too bright. It's hard for me to stay cool.

Phyto: Well, I for one happen to need the sun, and besides, it's about time somebody shed some light on what's been going on. I was wondering if any of you guys had noticed how many more plants have been dying in the shallow parts of the lake over the last five years? Things are happening to this lake!

Truttie: Hey, I've been worried too! Last year in my school we hardly had any new babies, and some of the ones we did have came out strange—with weird fins, and some without eyes! We've got to do something!

Mander: Mellow out dude! I don't see what you're all so worked up about. Up at the north end of the lake, where I come from, everything's been fine. Just relax and it'll all work out O.K.

Sal: Yeah, right! How long since you've seen your relatives at the south end? We're not as bad off as Truttie and the trout, but we're running out of food. Speaking of food, why don't you come on down here and speak your mind Flitters. (licks his/her lips)

Flitters: Help! He wants to have me for lunch—as if I didn't have enough problems already! This all sounds so awful! What can we do? What can we do? This sounds terrible! Doom and gloom! Doom and gloom!

Perch: Hey look, somebody's always telling us the world is going to end and we're all going to die because of this or that problem—but we always survive. My family has lived here for generations, and we've seen these things come and go. Remember the drought seven years ago, when everything dried up? And remember the frog that told us we were all going to shrivel up . . . he shut up pretty fast when the rains finally came.

Truttie: Yeah, but have you ever seen babies born without fins and eyes before? I'm telling you that unless we do something quick, we'll all be doomed.

Perch: Leave it to you, Truttie, to think the worst.

Phyto: Quit bickering. This is no way to solve a problem.

Mander: Problem? Problem? I don't see any problem. If we just let nature take care of itself . . .

Rocky: Wait a minute, may I speak? I've also noticed lots of strange things happening around here lately. For one thing, the fishing doesn't seem nearly as good as it was years ago. But the problem's not just in the lake. Take a close look at the trees and bushes in the forest—a lot of them are turning brown and dying too. At my job I get to hear what the "Two-Legs" in the houses around here talk about, you know, when they're not yelling at me and chasing me away from their garbage cans (Rocky chuckles). Let me tell you, they're pretty worried about this thing they call **ACID RAIN.**

Flitters: (quickly) **ACID RAIN**? What's that? What's that? It sounds scary!

Truttie: Sounds deadly!

Sal: Sounds hot!

Mander: Sounds cool!

Flitters: Does it burn?

Truttie: Does it sting?

Phyto: Will I wilt?

Perch: Quit panicking, and let the raccoon answer.

Rocky: Well I don't know too much about it, but I do know that it's got something to do with bad rain coming out of the sky. And all that smoke we see from the cars and factories, that seems to make the rain go bad, or something.

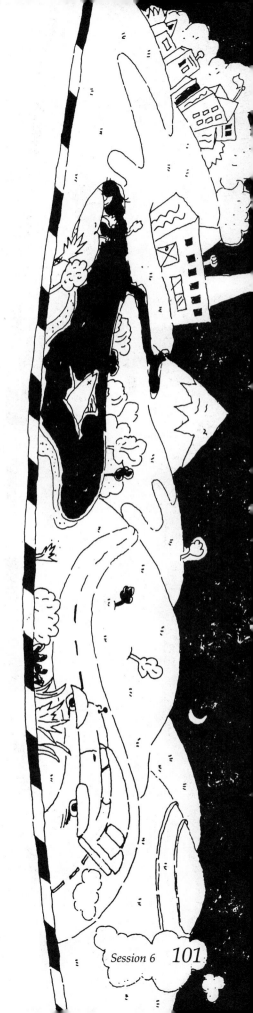

Truttie: (almost yelling) I knew it! I knew it! We'll all be killed! I'll bet none of you has seen any of my cousins, the carp, recently. That's because they've all been killed off. And (starts to sob) we'll be next! I'm tired of all these "Two-Legs" dirty tricks, and I can't survive below pH 6!

Perch: Good riddance! Those ugly old carp used to always take the best food anyway. I sure don't miss 'em.

Phyto: Things may seem good for you right now, Perch. But remember how we water plants thought that the sewage getting dumped in the lake last year was great? We ate the extra nutrients, partied, grew, and spread out all over the place. It wasn't till we started dying off by the thousands and our rotting plant bodies took away the oxygen in the water that we realized there was a serious problem. With us pulling out oxygen you were all in trouble, and I seem to remember that it was the "ugly old carp" that cleaned up that mess by eating the extra water plants.

Perch: Yes, but I happen to like what grows out of the nutrients the rotting plants left behind, and I don't mind if the oxygen is low. As for acid— if you can't take the pH, for goodness sake, get out of the lake! As for me, I can even survive at four point five!

Sal: Well macho fish, you might be able to handle more acid in the short term, but, like Phyto said, without plants and oxygen and other animals, Perch the perch will have no perch. You'll be left in the lurch! We're all in this thing together! (Sal turns to Rocky) I'd like to know if Rocky has heard anything about how those "Two-Legs" are going to fix this acid rain thing. After all, they seem to have caused it!

Mander: (interrupting) Look! I really don't know what you're all so worried about. I mean chill out, don't get carried away. Things will work out fine, just like they have in the past. Just because a few of us are having a hard time doesn't mean it won't get better.

Sal: (not at all convinced) Sure, "don't get carried away" — just wait till they carry you away — no thanks!

Rocky: I've heard the "Two-Legs" talking about something called buffer—they say that it will fix up the bad acid that keeps coming in with the rain.

Flitters: Oh, no! Not more chemicals! I've had enough of chemicals!

Truttie: And what do they plan on doing, just keep dumping in chemicals for as long as the acid rain keeps falling? How about stopping the pollution that causes it in the first place? Does buffer really work?

Rocky: I don't know, but I suppose it's a short-term solution at least, if they decide to treat our lake, that is.

Flitters: I hope they do, I mean maybe they won't, I mean what if they don't, oh I just don't know if they will or they won't . . .

Phyto: If they don't maybe we'll just have to do it ourselves. Like Rocky said, at least it'll help in the short-run.

Perch: And that'll give us some time to work things out. After all, let's not jump to any conclusions. We're not even sure this is caused by acid rain — that's just some word Rocky picked up when he was digging around in "Two-Leg" garbage cans. In any case, I think there's plenty of time.

Truttie: I don't think we've got much time at all, Perch. One of our cousins moved here last week from another lake down the hill. She says that their lake is completely dead already.

Perch: You mean Lower Lake? Hey, I have lots of friends down there . . .

Truttie: You *had* lots of friends down there, Perch.

Mander: (interrupting) Look, I really don't know what you're all so worried about. Like I said, up at my end of the lake . . .

Phyto: (losing patience) Will someone keep that Salamander quiet!?! (resumes calm tone) Now everybody, we've got lots of work to do. Maybe we could start by testing all the different parts of the lake to see how much acid there is. Does anybody have any Universal Indicator? Do you think we need to test the substrate? The sooner begun, the sooner done—let's get to work!

Manufacturers

We'd like to propose the solution of having scientists do research to help develop **acid-resistant fish.** These new hybrid fish could then be stocked in the lake along with perch and other fish that are better able to withstand the effects of acid rain. Then there would be fish for the fishing people and local residents to catch. We would not have to worry about the fish dying. In these modern times, we should have modern acid-resistant fish. Adapt or perish, that's what we say.

While adding buffer to lake water is a solution some have tried, we would like to propose the solution of **seeding the rain clouds with buffer.** In this way acid could be neutralized before it falls to earth.

We'd like to propose that the local residents **conserve energy.** If they would stop driving their cars as much, heat their houses less, and use fewer electrical gadgets, then less pollution would be made, and the problem of acid rain would be reduced. In order to make people conserve energy, we propose new taxes on gasoline, heating oil, and electricity. People will only cut back on luxuries if it hurts them financially.

Politicians

We'd like to propose the solution of building taller **smokestacks.** The gases produced by our factories could then be released high in the atmosphere and be blown away from our small town and lake. Acid rain would not be a problem for us anymore.

We'd also like to propose that an **emergency working committee** be set up, with representatives from all concerned groups, as well as a scientific consultant. This committee would be chaired by the Mayor. The committee would handle this crisis on a day-to-day basis and report weekly to the town council and issue news bulletins or other communications to keep the entire town informed of progress.

We further propose that a blue ribbon panel be formed, whose task is to review the problem of car exhaust. While the catalytic converters that people have on their cars and the smog certificates that they must get each year are a start, apparently the standards are not strict enough. Car exhaust still creates nearly half of the air pollutants in our region, and we believe this must stop. Perhaps the panel will suggest that we invest our tax money in the **invention of a special technology to reduce the amount of gases that are produced from cars.** In any case, the problem of reducing car exhaust must be solved and it is our hope that a panel of experts could best tell us how to achieve this.

Fishing People

We'd propose that the manufacturers hire more scientists to **take some of the sulfur and nitrogen out of the gases that are produced in their smokestacks.** Since acid rain is produced by oxides of sulfur and oxides of nitrogen, reducing the sulfur and nitrogen in the gases would reduce the amount of acid rain produced. If, by next year, each manufacturer does not comply with this new standard, they would have to pay large fines.

We'd like to propose that power plants and factories **use fuels that are naturally low in sulfur.** These fuels produce many fewer oxides of sulfur and therefore reduce the problem of acid rain. Of course there is a limit to the amount of low-sulfur coals that exist, but there should be enough for us to burn in our lifetimes. Maybe by the time it's all used up, we would have come up with another solution.

We'd like to propose that an **emergency report** on the acid rain situation be written and distributed free to all residents of the town. We've worked with several biologists, chemists, and environmental scientists in studying the effects of acid rain on the fish, and we think all residents should have access to up-to-date scientific information on acid rain. In addition, the booklet could include summaries of what other communities have done about acid rain. Intelligent decisions can be made only by informed citizens.

Local Residents

We'd like to propose that **more solar, wind and hydroelectric power be developed for this area, instead of burning coal, oil, and gasoline.** Burning fossil fuels creates oxides of sulfur and nitrogen, but using energy from the sun, wind, and water is clean. Because these forms of energy are more expensive, we propose that our politicians help develop a special national fund to help manufacturers and private citizens pay for converting homes and factories so they may begin using alternative forms of energy. This fund can also be used to help upgrade energy-conserving equipment, such as insulation and low-electricity light bulbs. We believe that, in doing this, our region could become a model in the widescale development and use of these new types of alternative energy generation.

We call for the establishment of an **independent commission** to monitor the progress of efforts against acid rain and make recommendations to the town council. This commission would have equal representation from the major local interest groups and town residents. It would also have a budget, to allow for the hiring of outside consultants.

We propose that necessary funds be found to conduct a **study of the plants and animals** in our region, paying particular attention to any changes taking place as a result of acid rain. Perhaps high school students could take this on as a project, under the direction of local biologists.

We think it would be helpful to have educators from the local junior college and the science center prepare some **lessons on acid rain** for students from early elementary through high school. These could include science experiments, role-playing activities, and reading current news articles, so our young people will know about this problem and be better prepared to deal with it.

Session 7: Town Meeting: Making Community Decisions

Overview

The problem of acid rain is, above all else, about making decisions. All too often, science classes deal with the "facts," while real-life decisions are left for the social studies classroom. Increasingly we are learning that the world does not make such distinctions—scientific understanding and social discussion/decision-making need to go hand in hand, if many of our most pressing environmental and technological problems are to be solved.

In this session, your gavel calls to order the "Emergency Town Meeting on Acid Rain," and your students, representing four major interest groups in the imaginary community of Laketown, state their views and discuss possible solutions. The emphasis is on structured discussion aimed at refining and reflecting upon suggestions for solving the problems caused by acid rain.

The simulated town meeting is not meant to be a literal representation of what really happens at a town meeting. The primary purpose of the format is to give students a structure within which to sort through, express, and refine scientific and social information. To this end, the usual meeting rules and procedures should be adapted in whatever ways best serve your educational goals.

At the end of the session, students should have a clearer sense of how they personally feel and think about the problem of acid rain. They should also have enough confidence in their own knowledge and outlook to follow the issue further, as active participants in future decisions about acid rain and other environmental and technology-related issues.

To be most effective, the town meeting discussion needs to be clearly structured, particularly with a class that has less experience with this type of activity. Provide clear and specific instructions at each stage. Set firm time limits, to make sure the open-ended nature of some of the activity doesn't take needed time away from later parts. The discussion should have a definite conclusion, with the class being given the opportunity to suggest a range of solutions that might be acceptable to the whole group (they will be able to express how they feel about these solutions in Session 8).

In regard to timing, suggestions for each segment are included in parentheses, assuming a 50-minute class session. However, if your class has done similar activities before and can move at a different pace, or you wish to modify the time frame to suit your own situation, by all means do so. It is important to make sure that the preparation period for interest groups just prior to the meeting does not exceed five minutes, to make sure there is time for the meeting.

Obviously, the conduct, organization, depth, and tone of the town meeting will vary greatly, depending on the particular class. Some teachers may want to make the town meeting aspect of this unit a more long-term class project, involving the student interest teams in more preparation, outside reading and research, and more elaborate presentations and debates. In such a case, the questions concerning "democracy" raised by some students, such as "why can't one of us be Mayor?" and the more complex (and socially accurate) process of lobbying, can be considered over a longer time frame, and, in that case, it might be that a student (or students) could play a leadership role at the meeting, instead of the teacher. In general, feel free to modify and extend the meeting format as you think most useful and rewarding for your students.

The purposes of the session are to: (1) prompt students to recall what they have learned about acid rain in the context of group discussions; (2) encourage students to synthesize knowledge and ideas to produce a coherent presentation from a particular point of view; and (3) give students experience suggesting solutions, modifying them in response to other ideas, and presenting them in a revised form to seek wider agreement.

What You Need

For the class:
☐ 4 sheets of butcher paper
☐ masking tape

For each group of four students:
☐ 5 sentence strips (see "Getting Ready," Session 1, for information on making or obtaining sentence strips)
☐ 1 marking pen

Getting Ready

Before the Day of the Activity

1. Read over the group notes and possible solutions the students turned in at the end of Session 6, and make comments as needed. These will be returned to the interest groups during the first part of this session.

2. You may want to do some extra preparation for the town meeting, such as making a banner to hang in the classroom announcing a "Laketown Emergency Town Meeting on Acid Rain" and/or place cards for each of the groups.

On the Day of the Activity:

1. Select and prepare a space on one wall of the room where the town meeting interest groups can post their solution strips.

2. Organize the seating in the room into a semi-circular or other meeting-like arrangement. Try to avoid rows of seats where interest groups can't see each other clearly. This is especially important for the discussion of each group's presentation.

Introduce the Town Meeting (5 minutes)

1. Introduce the session by saying something to this effect: "As you are aware, a number of interest groups have been preparing their points of view for the emergency town meeting on acid rain."

"In my capacity as mayor of Laketown, I have invited these groups to this town meeting, to listen to the different points of view, and see if we can find some common solutions to the acid rain problem that affects our community."

"In a few minutes, each of the groups will tell us who they are and why they have come to the town meeting. But first I will explain the meeting procedure and then give you five minutes for final meeting preparations."

2. Explain the meeting procedure as follows:

   a. Each group in turn will be asked to explain who they are, how they see the issue of acid rain, and what solutions they would like to propose. They will have 3 minutes per group to do this.

   b. Immediately after a group's presentation, the other groups have a chance to ask questions of or make brief comments about what the presenting group has said (2 minutes per group).

   c. The presenting group will be allowed to make a brief response to these questions or comments (1 minute per group).

   d. After all presentations are completed, each group will meet again to think of solutions to the acid rain problem which they believe might be more acceptable to some or all of the groups at the meeting.

To clarify the time frame, you may want to link the questions or comments from the other groups with the presenting group's responses, and allow a total of three minutes for this, for each of the four presentations. You will probably want to have the presenting group respond to questions or comments as they arise, rather than waiting until after all questions and comments to make a response. In either case, allow approximately three minutes.

Final Preparation of Group Presentations (5 minutes)

1. Remind each group that, during the first part of the town meeting, they are to present three things:

> a. A brief description of who they are and what they do. (Example: "We represent the (*type of group*) in Laketown, and we (*what they do*)."

> b. A statement of how the group see the issue of acid rain, including how it affects them, and what possible solutions they can think of that will help solve their problems (and possibly those of other groups as well).

> c. At least two questions or statements they would like to direct to two of the other groups. (You might need to give the students some examples, such as, "We as politicians would like to ask the manufacturers if they are willing to donate some money to acid rain research?" or "We as local residents think that the fishing people should have stricter quotas put on commercial fishing.")

2. Emphasize that the groups should try to come up with well-thought-out statements about their group's point of view, and avoid unnecessary name-calling or hostility. A reference here to the previous discussion about the constructive and non-constructive attitudes of the animals in the play might be helpful.

3. Have students assemble in their town meeting interest groups (as in the previous session). Redistribute the notes each group made in Session 6 (along with your comments) and let them begin final preparations.

4. As the groups prepare, circulate to answer questions and help evaluate or refine points of view. You may also want to use this time to plan the order of group presentations, consulting with the groups as you wish.

Student Presentations & Responses
(25 minutes)

1. Regain the attention of the class. Call the meeting to order. (If you have a gavel, use it!) Announce that you, as the Mayor, have called this town meeting because many people are very concerned about the effects of acid rain in Laketown and the surrounding area. You have invited several of the groups in the community who have an interest in the acid rain problem.

2. In whatever order you deem appropriate, have each group make their presentations. They should also field questions and comments from the other groups immediately after their presentation. Limit these to brief interchanges in order to keep up the momentum of the meeting.

3. You may want to help clarify some of the points and questions being raised, especially when they are somewhat rambling or not fully thought out, by rephrasing them on behalf of the groups offering them.

4. Endeavor to keep each group to the allotted time, and continue to remind the class that the purpose of the meeting is to look for common ground between the different interest groups.

Town Meeting: Brainstorming Solutions
(10 minutes)

1. Explain to the class that they will now meet again in their groups to discuss new or revised solutions they believe will address the concerns of several or all of the interest groups. (In keeping with the role of Mayor, you could say something like: "Now that the initial presentations have been made, I think it would be constructive for each of the interest groups to caucus, or hold brief discussions among themselves, to come up with solutions they think can gain wide acceptance."

Caucus is a much-used word in American politics, usually relating to political conventions. It can refer more generally to a gathering of local members of a political party to nominate candidates and delegates, or to a meeting of members of a particular party or interest group to decide upon actions they believe should be taken in a larger legislative body or at a convention. The word is probably Native-American in origin, related to the word in the Algonquian language for "advisor."

If there is time, you may want to have the groups choose and list the three solutions their group likes best of all those proposed. Then have each group prioritize their list, in 1, 2, 3 order. The Mayor can then say that the highest priority solutions on each list will be given extensive consideration, and committees will be appointed to begin investigating the feasibility of implementing them. Then the meeting is adjourned. Adding this component may help provide a sense of completion to the meeting.

One way to make a transition might be to tell the students that the solutions proposed in the town meeting are going to refined and voted on by a mass meeting of all townspeople, during the next session. At that mass meeting, the students will not be representing any particular interest group, but will instead vote for the solutions they personally believe to be the most appropriate and effective.

2. Tell the groups that when they think they have come up with some broadly acceptable solutions, they should write them in large letters on strips of paper you will provide.

3. Hand out the strips of paper and marking pens, and tell the groups to begin discussing solutions.

4. Circulate among the groups, to help clarify issues and solutions, and to carry ideas between groups. At the end of five minutes (or before, if they have finished) ask all of the groups to post their solution strips on the wall.

Acid Rain: The Next Step (5 minutes)

1. Inform the class that the town meeting is now adjourned. As Mayor, you may want to thank all the participants for their attention and concern. You might also add that the solutions proposed will be considered by various town committees, and recommendations for action will be made to another town meeting sometime in the future. As Mayor of Laketown, you promise to do all you can to arrive at constructive and effective ways to deal with the problem as soon as possible.

2. Make a transition, in whatever way you think best, away from the roles in the town meeting, and back to the students' own opinions. Explain that in the last session of this acid rain unit they will examine, **from their own points of view,** the various solutions that have been proposed. Each person in the class will get a chance to think about how they really feel about each of the solutions suggested, outside of the roles they have been playing in the town meeting.

3. Add that the class will also consider again the statements and questions they listed in the first session of the unit, to see what still needs to be clarified and what new questions have arisen. Ideas about other ways to find out more about the effects of acid rain can also be raised. Ask them to think of any issues or questions they might want to discuss before the unit ends.

Acid Rain East and West

Harte-Hoffman Study Is First Evidence Acid Rain Is Affecting Animals in the Rockies

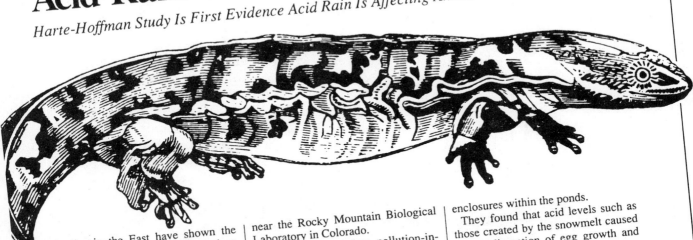

Studies in the East have shown the impact of acid rain on fish populations and its probable cause of some amphibian declines, but a study by physicist John Harte, professor of energy and resources, is the first strong evidence that similar impacts may now be hitting some animal populations in the West.

Harte's research reported results of an eight-year study in the Colorado Rockies, linking seasonal increases in acid precipitation with declines of a well-established salamander population.

The continuing research project combines long-term population studies and environmental monitoring with in-field experiments on pollution-induced acidification.

Harte's team discovered a strong association between steep declines in natural populations of hardy Rocky Mountain salamanders and increases in acidification in their ponds due to acid rain and snow.

Harte's collaborator on the research project is Erika Hoffman, a scientist at Lawrence Berkeley Laboratory. Their project has been carried out since 1981 at high mountain ponds in a watershed near the Rocky Mountain Biological Laboratory in Colorado.

Unlike the long-term pollution-induced acid level increases in the East, acidification in these high mountain regions of the West is seasonal, triggered by high acid-level snow melting into the pond basins in late spring, Harte explained. When snowmelt runs into the ponds, a "pulse" of acidity hits the aquatic habitat, Harte explained.

It is when the timing of the acid pulse coincides with sensitive periods of egg development that the acidification can be most devastating to survival, Harte and Hoffman found.

"The standard acid-level measurements used by EPA, based on mid-summer lake acidity levels, just aren't relevant to these pond dwellers in the Rockies. The peak acidity levels here are over by then," Harte said.

Harte and Hoffman studied populations of a long-lived species of amphibians known as tiger salamanders. These six-inch-long creatures normally live about 10 years, but don't reproduce for at least the first few years.

The Berkeley scientists counted adults and eggs during the spring and summer, and recorded acid levels of 14 Rocky Mountain ponds where the salamanders lived and bred. They also studied the effects of the measured acid levels on samples of the amphibians in enclosures within the ponds.

They found that acid levels such as those created by the snowmelt caused severe disruption of egg growth and killed developing embryos.

The study does not prove that acidification is causing the salamander declines they measured, Harte and Hoffman point out. But it does show that the levels of acidification that the creatures are exposed to can be lethal if the pulse coincides with early egg development, as it often does.

"There are probably many causes of population declines worldwide," Harte said. "In some cases it is probably acid precipitation from pollution; in others it may be disruptions of the habitat or even pathogens.

"The importance of this meeting is to ...see if the declines are merely periodic fluctuations or if there is some pattern.

"If there is a pattern, we should redouble our efforts to identify the causes and to change what conditions we can so that populations do not decline further toward extinction, and so that other species do not suffer from environmental degradation."

The team's work was reported in February at a special scientific meeting called by the National Research Council to explore reports of sharp declines in amphibian populations at pristine sites worldwide. —*Wallace Ravven*

Reprinted from the *Berkeleyan*, a newspaper for faculty and staff of the University of California at Berkeley.

Session 8: "Everything You've Always Wanted To Know About Acid Rain . . .

Overview

This final session provides an opportunity for your students to consider and discuss their own opinions about solutions to the problems posed by acid rain. The solutions suggested at the town meeting are refined and straw votes taken. Of course, these are not meant to be definitive decisions—no one has yet come up with a comprehensive answer to the problems posed by acid rain. The suggested solutions give each student a chance to compare the range of ideas represented in the class with their own current opinion.

During the latter part of the session the list of questions and statements about acid rain begun in the first session is re-examined, to clarify concepts or issues that may have been overlooked during previous discussion, to give students and teacher some measure of ways in which understandings have grown, and to generate further questions from their new found knowledge.

The purposes of this session are to: (1) give students more experience suggesting and modifying solutions; (2) provide an opportunity for each student to think through what their current personal thoughts and feelings are about acid rain and proposed solutions, and compare their ideas to the opinions of classmates; (3) review the list of student questions and statements, to clarify any continuing misconceptions or uncertainties students may have about the scientific or social issues of acid rain; (4) provide the teacher and the students with feedback on what has been learned and clarified from the unit; (5) communicate to students that questions are a key part of the search for understanding, and are generated in all phases of learning.

What You Need

For the class:
- ☐ 10 extra sentence strips
- ☐ 1 marking pen
- ☐ "Solution Strips" generated in Session 7
- ☐ List of statements and questions begun in Session 1

Getting Ready

Before the Day of the Activity

Read over the possible solutions that students wrote on paper strips in Session 7. You may want to sort these into groups; for example: based on their similarities, or because they are alternatives, or because they address the same issue; etc. You may also want to involve the students in this process at the beginning of the session, if you have time.

On the Day of the Activity

If they are not up already, post the list of solutions generated in Session 7, and the lists of student statements and questions compiled in Session 1.

Sorting Out Solutions

1. Direct the attention of the class to the list of suggested solutions that were compiled by the interest groups in the previous session. Ask them to assess, as individuals, **not** as part of an interest group, what they think of each of the suggested solutions to the acid rain problem. You may need to remind them to focus on their own thoughts, and not be swayed by their town meeting roles. One way to do this might be to ask, "If you were President, what would you do about acid rain?"

2. Invite students to suggest any solutions they think are broadly acceptable to the class, or to briefly propose other solutions that might be generally acceptable. Ask them to outline why they think the solutions are likely to meet with approval. Write any new suggestions that you consider reasonable on separate solution strips and post them with the others (or invite the students who propose them to do so).

3. Depending on the number and type of proposed solutions, you may want or need to assist the class in refining and combining them to narrow down the list. A very large number of solutions, while demonstrating that there are many approaches to the problem, might cause the voting to take too long. In some cases, two very similar solutions can be naturally combined.

4. Encourage critical assessment of the proposed solutions by asking questions such as: "Would this be an expensive solution?" "Who would bear the costs?" "Does this solution seem to be scientifically sound?" "Would it be fair to the average citizen? the business community?" "What would be the next step?"

5. After a number of solutions have been listed and selected for voting, tell the class that you now are going to conduct a straw poll. Explain that you'd like the students to vote on each solution on the final list according to their own personal views.

6. Explain the rules for voting as follows: "If you agree strongly with the solution suggested, raise both of your arms, holding your hands together. If you agree, but have some reservations about the solution, raise one hand only. If you are not sure, and want to pass, cross your arms. And if you disagree, put your hand out in front of you, with your thumbs down." Every person should vote on each solution.

7. One at a time, read out the proposed solutions and poll the class on each of them. It's probably not necessary to count each of the responses, rather, summarize what sort of response you can see from the front, e.g., "A few of you strongly agree, most agree with reservations, and only three actually disagree." Write a brief summary of the voting pattern next to each solution, e.g.,"Most agree, with reservations, to this solution."

7. You may want to discuss with the class the importance of being able to study and analyze all sides of an issue, and to hear opposing viewpoints, before making decisions. At the same time, it is very important that citizens have a sense of their own power to make decisions—it is up to everyone to gain an understanding of the issues and realize their personal responsibility to take part in decision-making processes. Issues that affect us all, whether they involve acid rain and global warming, or political alliances and economic directions, are not "best left to the experts." Technical expertise is sorely needed and must be taken into account, but it is the general population and their elected representatives that make the decisions. Ideally, that is what democracy is all about.

In some classes of younger students, teachers have summarized the votes using a simple drawing of a face, with a smile indicating total agreement, a frown for total disagreement, and a range of expressions between to signify a more mixed response.

Love Canal refers to a toxic chemical waste dump in Niagara, New York. 22,000 tons of toxic waste had been buried in an unused canal near homes and directly under a school. In 1978, Ms. Lois Marie Gibbs, then a housewife with no prior community organizing experience, connected the severe health problems suffered by her own two children and other neighborhood families to the toxic waste. She organized a neighborhood association and led community efforts that resulted in a governmental cleanup effort and the evacuation and relocation of over 800 families. Love Canal became infamous, symbolic of the many serious problems posed by toxic chemical waste. Ms. Gibbs went on to form the Citizen's Clearinghouse for Hazardous Waste, an informational center based in Arlington, Virginia that works with 3,000 community groups nationwide. In 1990 she was one of six grass-roots activists honored worldwide for their efforts on behalf of the environment by the Goldman Environmental Foundation of San Francisco.

In her book, "Love Canal: My Story" she writes of her initial door-to-door petition campaign, "I had never done anything like this . . . I was afraid a lot of doors would be slammed in my face . . . I was afraid of making a fool of myself . . . Then I thought: But what's more important—what people think or your child's health?" More than 150 people signed the petition; no one slammed a door in her face.

8. Point out that a majority vote on issues of the environment may not necessarily be the best way, and is definitely not the only way, of making decisions. In some cases, when a small group of people in a community is much more adversely affected than others, other measures besides a majority vote may be needed to prevent serious damage. The terrible chemical pollution at Love Canal is just one case in point. In other cases, standards already set by federal or state agencies may be violated, and the issue is taken directly to the courts, rather than the voters. And in many cases that seem to affect certain communities, but later turn out to affect all of us, the issue is often first called to our attention, not by a vote or an official, but by a few individuals who start studying and raising the issue in the mass media and books, or through protests and demonstrations. Finally, in regard to coming up with and deciding on solutions to problems like acid rain, remind the class that, regardless of what we might want to do, our environment has the ultimate power of veto—it may not want to do what we *vote* it should!

9. Stress that, to be workable, solutions must be based on a good understanding of the problem. Acid rain and its effects, like many other environmental problems, is not fully understood. As new knowledge is gained and more data is gathered, solutions also change.

What We Know and Wonder Now

1. Point out to your students that their understanding of acid rain has probably changed over the course of the unit. One way to get a sense of this is to reexamine the list of statements and questions begun on the first day of the unit.

2. Ask the class to focus their attention first on the list of statements representing what they had "heard" about acid rain. Are there any statements on the list that are incorrect or only partially correct?

3. Then focus the attention of the class on the list of questions that were generated as the unit progressed. Which questions were answered or partially answered through what was done and learned in the unit? What additional questions does the class have that should be added to the list? You may want to write the following quotations on the board, to emphasize that good questions are at the base of good science.

> *"The outcome of any serious research can only be to make two questions grow where only one grew before."*
>
> —*Thorstein Veblen*

> *"Not only does science begin in wonder, it also ends in wonder."*
>
> —*Abraham Maslow*

4. If there is time, you might want to encourage the students to brainstorm ideas about imagined experiments that could be done to find out the answers to some of their questions or to design new technologies for solving the problem of acid rain.

5. Reiterate that, as information about acid rain changes, the questions we have about it and the solutions we propose are also likely to change. You might want to point out the main things you think the class has learned from the unit on acid rain, or encourage students to do so.

6. Encourage the class to keep reading and thinking about acid rain—the solutions are still unfolding, and with the information they have gained in this unit, they may be able play an important part in deciding what should be done about it in the future.

You may want to take some time and gather some resources in this session, or most likely for later extensions, for students to work together to seek more information about some of the questions on the class list that remain unanswered. Teams of students could do library research and write summaries of the new information gained for reports to the class.

Going Further

The following are just a few of many possible extension ideas for this unit. Several ideas that relate specifically to buffers and neutralization are listed following Session 2, on page 35. The GEMS staff would very much welcome hearing about the other extension ideas of you and your students.

Mystery Lakes

Set up a more complex series of "mystery" lakes with a wider variety of pH's, by making various dilutions of the acid rain solution. Give each lake an appropriate name, perhaps relating to your locality. Have your students determine the pH of each lake using Universal Indicator solution.

High school chemistry students, with an understanding of molarity, can determine the more precise pH of these mystery lakes, as well as their buffering capacities, by using standard titration techniques.

Lake County

Make up a map to be used as a focus for class discussion on which you draw a series of small lakes, factories, cities, and perhaps some larger bodies of water, mountains, or other physical features. Select a particular pH for each lake on the map (or have these lakes represent the mystery lakes mentioned in the previous activity, and have students determine the pH themselves).

When you choose the pH for each lake on the map, think about the potential factors of: location of urban areas and factories, wind direction, foliage, and soil type. For instance, you might want to name one of the lakes, Granite Lake, and assign it a low pH, or you might have a Pine Forest Lake with a relatively low pH. You may want to include some discrepant pH values, for instance a lake near an urban area with a high pH. You could further complicate the scenario by having the map extend across an international border, and include several very acid lakes on one side of the border that are clearly the result of industrial pollution from the other country.

Challenge students to write a story about the region, which explains why each lake has a certain pH. Encourage them to be creative (for example, by including stories of forest fires that renewed the buffering capacities of lakes in the area of the fire). If your students need more guidance, you might give them a list of factors to consider, such as which direction the prevailing wind blows, and what soil types exist in the region.

Don't Rain on My Piazza

Set up an open-ended experiment in which students investigate the effect of acid on various materials, such as: brick, nylon, styrofoam, colored paper, concrete, marble, limestone, wood, cotton, plastics, cellulose (leaves), and so on. While most of these materials will be inert with "safer" pH's, you may wish to set up a demonstration of the effect of an acid of higher molarity on materials like nylon or polyester. Students could determine the safest material to wear in class. You could set up a "museum" with displays of the results, for other classes to stroll through.

Acid Money

A striking way of demonstrating the effects of acidic corrosion on metals (paralleling the effects of acid rain on bridges, water pipes, and other metal structures) is to expose coins to full-strength vinegar. Place paper towelling in the bottom of plastic cups, then add several coins to each cup. You may want to compare pennies, nickels, dimes, and quarters. Just barely cover the coins with a thin layer of full-strength vinegar, to allow oxygen to get to the coins. Cover the cups with plastic wrap and wait several days. Blue and green deposits indicate the presence of copper and nickel that has corroded from the metal and changed into non-metallic form.

Acid Authors

Invite your students to write their own play about acid rain, perhaps inspired by the play in Session 6. One group might want to start by writing another act to the play that appears in the guide. This next act might take place two years later, and could further develop the characters as they make a group decision about how best to take care of their environment or what responses they have to the buffer treatment of their lake. Or, you could specify different settings and scenarios, for example, having an 8th grade class take over the White House and set nationwide policy on acid rain! The group could also present the play to the class and/or other classes. Your students will probably have lots of good suggestions for plays—list all their ideas and let groups or individuals each pick one to develop further. There are wonderful opportunities here for interdisciplinary work with teachers of Language Arts, English, or Drama classes.

The same applies to short stories or newspaper articles. One group may want to make a facsimile edition of a newspaper. This could be a newspaper of the future and acid rain is in the headlines.

Maybe the newspaper reports that the worst acid rainstorm on record has just taken place—or maybe some futuristic new measures to control pollution have just been announced. Again, draw on the creativity of your students to make these writing projects exciting and meaningful.

As a class or team project, your students could also write and desktop-publish an "Acid Rain Factsheet" for schoolwide distribution, or for inclusion in the school or local community group newsletter.

The Plight of the Tiger Salamander

Suggest that your students conduct library research on the plight of the tiger salamander, a suspected victim of acid rain. As they discover other kinds of animals or plants threatened by acid rain, they may want to make a large chart depicting the endangered organisms, including drawings and relevant facts about their life histories.

The Rain in Spain . . .

Have the class make an international map depicting the status of acid rain around the globe. Assign different student groups to investigate the acidity of rain in different continents, perhaps as a library assignment. Color in the "hot" spots on a large map. Use a different color to indicate the largest industrial areas. You might want to have students research and post other information, such as population densities, major wind directions, etc. As a class, see if you can notice patterns or generate hypotheses about why some areas have more acidic rain than others.

Real Lakes

Consider a special class project to field test a lake or lakes in your locality for acidity, over a given period of time and after rainstorms. You and your students could gather resource materials to assist you in planning this task, and then report on your findings in a school or community publication. Analyzing lake samples for acidity could also be the basis for an excellent science fair project. You may also want to invite an environmental scientist, hydrologist, other researcher, or person knowledgeable about the lakes in your region, to speak to the class, help answer additional questions about acid rain and its effects, and advise the class about methods for testing a local lake.

Behind the Scenes

This section is organized into three parts. It begins with a background discussion about acids, bases, buffers, acid rain, the problems it causes, and proposed solutions. This is followed, on page 137, by detailed information about collecting soil samples and, on page 141, by instructions for preparing a 1 molar sulfuric acid solution.

Part 1: Introduction

This unit is designed so your students can learn about the causes and effects of acid rain, and discuss potential solutions, without needing to have previous knowledge of chemistry. Early in the unit (Session 2) several chemistry concepts are introduced to the students, including: a functional definition of acids, bases, and neutrals; that there are acids (and bases) of different strengths; how one measures the strength of an acid (or base); and how the pH scale is used to quantify the relative strengths of acids, bases, and neutrals. The GEMS unit *Of Cabbages and Chemistry* provides a series of activities that can be used to introduce students to the concepts of acids, bases, and neutrals in a guided discovery fashion. Some teachers have found it useful to present the activities in *Of Cabbages and Chemistry* to their students **before** beginning the Acid Rain unit.

Whether or not you precede this unit with *Of Cabbages and Chemistry* or some other introduction to acid/base chemistry, your students are likely to have further questions about acids, pH, buffers, and neutralization. We have provided detailed information in this section to help you stretch your own knowledge of these concepts, so you can feel more comfortable answering students' questions. Consult a high school chemistry text for more information about acid/base chemistry.

You will also find some additional information about acid rain in this section. We have only included information necessary for you to adequately present the unit to your students. If you want to learn more about acid rain, we have suggested several references in the "Resources" section on page 142 in this guide. Keep in mind that much is still unknown about how acid rain forms, what effects it has, and which solutions are best. Scientists are discovering more about these topics all the time. We suggest that you and your students be on the alert for newspaper articles about acid rain. Up-to-date articles will hopefully contain information about the latest discoveries.

This background section is written for you, the teacher. **It is not meant to be read out loud to the class.** Information appropriate for student use is included in the class sessions and student readings. If you choose to introduce some of what is contained in this section to your students, we think that you will find it more effective to present the ideas **in your own words**, and only after students have had firsthand experience and a chance to discuss their own ideas and perceptions.

What is an acid?

Acids are a group of chemical substances that have similar properties when dissolved in water. Among these properties are sourness and the ability to: break up proteins, dissolve metals, and conduct electricity. Some common acids are: vinegar, battery acid, stomach acid, orange juice, cola and other carbonated beverages, tomatoes, coffee, and tea. Most plants are at least slightly acidic, including nearly all vegetables and fruit. Citric acid, malic acid, tartaric acid, oxalic acid, and ascorbic acid (Vitamin C) are the most common acids found in fruits and vegetables. The acid in car batteries is sulfuric acid. The acid in carbonated beverages is carbonic acid. The acid in our stomachs is hydrochloric acid. Formic acid is what causes an ant bite to itch.

Acids taste sour. One shared property of many acids is that they taste sour or astringent. As vegetables and fruits ripen, their acid content decreases. This is why ripe vegetables and fruit taste less tart or sour. While strong acids are not things we usually taste (!), most of us have had occasion to "taste" stomach acid (hydrochloric acid, a strong acid) when we've had the misfortune of "throwing up" the contents of our stomach. This unwitting experiment provides direct evidence of the sour taste of acids.

Acids destroy proteins. You may have gotten orange or tomato sauce on a canker sore or cracked lip and felt a stinging sensation. It is the acid in these substances that causes this stinging. In fact, acids *denature* or destroy proteins. This means that acids actually begin to disassemble protein molecules, causing them to uncoil and change shape. Our own bodies are protected from weak acids, such as those we eat, by our skin and, internally, by mucus coverings. However, when even a weak acid touches the unprotected tissue in a cut, or a sore (irritated) throat, we can feel the denaturing properties of acid at work.

While the acid in orange juice will not do serious damage, stomach acid is much stronger, and can actually eat a hole in your skin. Luckily, stomach acid rarely comes into contact with skin so it is not a problem. Our stomachs are protected from stomach acid by a layer of mucus. If stomach acid splashes up into the unprotected esophagus (as when the stomach is agitated, or over-filled with acid) the esophagus can become irritated, and we experience heartburn, sometimes called "acid stomach." If some of the protective coating of the stomach is eroded, the acid in the stomach will actually eat away the inner lining of the stomach, a condition we refer to as an ulcer.

Other, sometimes more helpful, examples of how acids denature proteins can be found in cooking. Lemon juice and bacteria that produce acid are used to curdle milk. Milk curdles when some of its proteins are denatured and then clump or coagulate together. This is the principle behind the production of some cheeses and other dairy products, such as yogurt. Vinegar and lemon juice are often used to tenderize meat. These acids act by partially breaking down the proteins that hold muscle fibers in the meat together. In some cultures, people eat raw fish that has been marinated in lemon juice. While raw fish can be hard to chew, the acid in the lemon juice makes the fish tender and easy to eat.

Acids dissolve metals. Acids are corrosive to most metals. The acid in tomato sauce will react with an aluminum pot, producing a discolored sauce tasting of aluminum! This is why some people choose not to use metal pots when cooking acidic foods, and why aluminum drink cans always have a plastic coating inside. Acid is also used to etch metals in industry and in various art applications, and even a slightly acidic domestic water supply can end up corroding copper pipes.

Acids also dissolve many other chemicals. For example, calcium carbonate in teeth can be dissolved by the acids produced by the bacteria in our mouths. To observe a similar reaction, try putting a hard-boiled egg, still in its shell, in vinegar. After several days the shell (made of calcium carbonate) will totally dissolve in the vinegar.

Acids conduct electricity. Acids do not just dissolve in water. They dissociate (break into separate chemical parts known as ions). Ions are particles with electrical charges. Ions can have either positive ($+$) or negative ($-$) charges. These charges allow electricity to move through a solution more readily than through a solution without charges. This is why car batteries contain acid. Flashlight batteries also contain charged chemicals, which are dissolved in a jelly that acts as a sort of "solidified solution." Some flashlight batteries are called alkaline batteries—these contain bases, the chemical counterpart of acids. *Bases* also contain many ions, and also conduct electricity well.

What is meant by "strong" and "weak" acids?

Not all acids are the same strength. Each has its own character; some are stronger, and some are weaker. An acid's strength is determined by its molecular structure. Acids that easily *dissociate* (break into ions) in water are considered to be "*strong acids.*" Those acids that dissociate less readily in water are classified as "*weak acids.*"

These terms can be confusing, as you can have a "strong acid" (such as sulfuric or battery acid) mixed with a large volume of water so that it becomes extremely dilute, but it would still be referred to as a "strong acid." Similarly, "weak acids" in a concentrated form can be very irritating, but they're still considered to be "weak."

One way of looking at this potentially confusing situation is to understand that, when strong acid is diluted with water, it can be made into a safe solution, because the concentration of acid ions in the solution becomes low. However, the character of the acid, as determined by the structure of each individual acid ion, does not change. Sulfuric acid, which is used in batteries and also found in acid rain, is always classified as a strong acid, no matter whether it is concentrated or dilute.

Whether or not a strong acid (or a weak acid) is dangerous depends on its concentration. The factors of *strength* and *concentration* can be easily confused by anyone, and are especially difficult to comprehend for students who have not reached a formal level of reasoning.

While strong acids can be more dangerous than weak acids, they are also often very useful. They are used, for example, in car batteries, because they are better conductors of electricity.

What makes an acid an acid?

A property all acids share is that when they are dissolved in water and dissociate, they release positive *hydrogen ions* (H+) into the solution. Hydrogen ions (H+) are sometimes referred to as *protons*. Substances that release protons (acids) are sometimes referred to as *proton donors*. Protons are powerful chemical agents that can attach to the molecules of another substance and cause them to change chemically, making acids an important chemical sub-group. It is these protons, or ions, that conduct electricity, dissolve metal, denature proteins, and produce a sour taste. The more readily an acid dissociates (releasing protons), the stronger it is. The stronger an acid is, the better it is at conducting electricity, dissolving metal, denaturing proteins, etc. The ions of dissociated acids can also take protons out of solution, by recombining with the protons. However, to be an acid, a substance must give more protons to a solution than it takes.

What about substances that aren't acids?

All substances can be classified as acids, *bases*, or *neutrals* (neither acid nor base). A base can be viewed as the chemical "opposite" of an acid, in that bases are substances that take more protons from a solution than they give. Bases are sometimes referred to as *proton acceptors*. In order to remove protons (H + or positive ions) from solution, bases typically have lots of negative ions. Common bases include ocean water, soap, baking soda, ammonia, and lye. Bases are sometimes referred to as alkaline. Neutrals have an equal balance of proton donors (positive ions) and proton acceptors (negative ions).

How do we measure whether something is acidic, basic or neutral?

The *pH scale* is an expanding yardstick that measures how acidic or basic a chemical is. The scale goes from 0 to 14. The number in the middle, 7, describes neutrals. Numbers less than 7 on the pH scale are used to denote acids. The lower the number, the stronger or more concentrated the acid, so, for example, a solution with a pH of 3 is more acidic (has more H + protons in it) than one with a pH of 5. Numbers greater than 7 are used to quantify bases. The higher the number, the stronger the base (the higher concentration of proton acceptors).

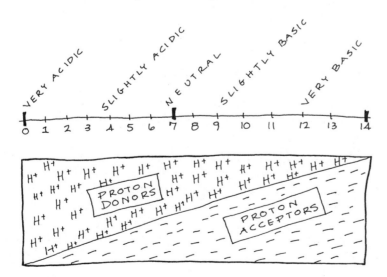

Technically, pH is calculated by determining the negative logarithm of the hydrogen ion concentration expressed in moles per liter of a given substance. The number of hydrogen ions in pure water is 10^{-7} moles per liter. By calculating the negative logarithm of 10^{-7} one arrives at a pH of 7.0 for water. One of the reasons for this calculation is to make miniscule quantities such as 10^{-7} into more easily usable numbers, like 7.

The abbreviation pH stands for *"the power of hydrogen,"* and it is a measure of the number of hydrogen ions or protons in a given volume of solution. Remembering that acids *release* hydrogen ions in a solution, and bases *remove* hydrogen ions from solution, it follows that low pH numbers have the highest power of hydrogen (or tendency to add hydrogen ions), whereas high pH numbers have the lowest power of hydrogen (because of their tendency to remove hydrogen ions from solution). Thus, acidity measured on a pH yardstick might be compared to an athletic competition; the person who comes in first in a competition places "better" (or more acidic!) than someone who places fourteenth. As the concentration of acidity (hydrogen ions or proton donors) decreases, the concentration of basicity (need for hydrogen ions or proton acceptors) in the substance increases. So a substance of pH 14 is a very strong base.

The pH scale is a *logarithmic scale*, like the Richter scale used to measure the extent of ground movement in earthquakes. This means that a substance of pH 6.0 is **ten times more acidic** than a substance of pH 7.0, a substance of pH 5.0 is **one hundred times more acidic** than a substance of pH 7.0, a substance of pH 4.0 is **one thousand times more acidic** than a substance of pH 7.0, and so on. Continuing with the athletic analogy, if the first place contestant ran the race in **1** second, then the person who placed second would run it in **10** seconds, the third place person in **100** seconds, the fourth place person in **1000** seconds, etc. The large time differences between each placement in this imaginary race are like the large differences in acidity between each pH unit. Or to put it another way, for every whole unit *decrease* in pH, there is a tenfold *increase* in the number of hydrogen ions. A solution of pH 4.0 will have 10 times the number of hydrogen ions as the same volume of a solution of pH 5.0.

How are acids neutralized?

Antacid tablets are made up of weak bases because, if the person took a strong base (proton acceptor) this might remove the protons from chemicals in cells and change them before the base got to the stomach where its antacid action is needed. For this reason, the medical treatment for an accident in which someone has swallowed a strong acid (or splashed it on their skin) is to administer lots of a weak base (or, if a weak base is not available, lots of water, which is a neutral substance).

Because of the chemically opposite nature of acids and bases, they can *neutralize* each other. This is why people with "acid stomachs" or heartburn will often drink a solution of baking soda (a weak base), or take a commercial "antacid." (Antacids are also weakly basic.) Remember that neutrals have a balance of proton donors (acid molecules) and proton acceptors (basic molecules). Thus, if you mix equal amounts of proton donors with proton acceptors, the donors donate and the acceptors accept, thereby producing a neutral solution. (Note: In reality, many bases don't take up *all* of the hydrogen ions, but if the number of hydrogen ions and proton acceptors are equal, then the solution is still said to be neutral.)

For example, when the excess acid in your stomach is neutralized by the base in an antacid tablet, most of the protons react with the proton acceptors in the base, until few, if any, are left unreacted. More often, the situation is one in which you have an unknown quantity of acid (such as in your stomach), and you add increments of base to progressively reduce the acidity (such as when you take some bicarbonate [baking soda] and then some more a bit later, until you no longer feel the effects of the excess acid in your stomach). In this case, you reduce the number of protons (because the base "accepts" and removes them) and therefore the concentration of acid. While you don't make a solution that is precisely neutral, you eventually neutralize most of the acid in the solution. Partially neutralizing an acid is often referred to as raising the pH (making it move toward the higher-numbered end of the scale); partially neutralizing a base is often referred to as lowering the pH.

Consider what happens when a tooth decays. Bacteria in our mouths produce acid, which in turn dissolves the calcium compound that makes up our teeth. Some people brush their teeth with baking soda in order to neutralize some of the acid in the mouth. Commercial toothpastes are also designed to raise the pH in the mouth environment, and contain chemicals that are similar to baking soda.

What happens to acid that has been neutralized?

When an acid is mixed with a base, the excess protons in the acid are taken in by the proton acceptors in the base, making two new products—water and a *salt*. This mixture of new products may look the same as the starting solutions, but it is chemically very different. For example, it is possible to take a high concentration of sulfuric acid (which would "burn" or denature your skin) and mix it with highly concentrated sodium hydroxide (the main chemical in some drain cleaners, which would also affect your skin) and produce a salt (sodium sulfate, commonly called Glauber's salt) and water. A similar mixture using hydrochloric acid would produce sodium chloride (table salt) and water.

Everyday usage of the word "salt" refers to table salt or sodium chloride. However, in chemical terminology, salt refers to compounds that contain at least one positive ion and one negative ion. Sodium chloride is one of many chemical salts. It is made of positive sodium ions ($Na+$) and negative chloride ions ($Cl-$), which are attracted together when there is no dissolving substance such as water to keep them apart, and form large ionic lattices, rather than single molecules. There are many household and industrial uses for chemical salts, explaining why acids and bases are commonly used in industrial plants.

Acid + Base = Salt + Water

This production of salt is one of the main reasons why bases are not used to neutralize acidified lakes. Adding excess salt changes the chemical environment in the lake, making it inhospitable to plants and animals.

What's a buffer?

Buffers are special chemicals that can change the pH of a solution toward a different, specific, predetermined pH. For example, you could have a pH 8 buffer, that when mixed with an acid solution of pH 4, would raise the pH (make it more basic). If enough of the buffer were added, the solution would become pH 8. If even more buffer were added, the solution would still remain pH 8. This same buffer, mixed with a basic solution of pH 10, would, with enough buffer, *lower* the pH to 8 (making it more acidic). No matter how much buffer was added, the solution would remain at pH 8. Different buffers are used to stabilize the pH of solutions at different specific pH values. Some stomach antacids are buffers. Buffers are added to fish tanks to help maintain the water at the specific pH that is best-suited to the requirements of the fish.

What is the pH of normal rain?

Even many thousands of years ago, long before our present problems of pollution and acid rain, all rainwater was slightly acidic. This natural acidity is mainly created as rain falls through the carbon dioxide gas in the atmosphere and forms carbonic acid. In Session 2 of this unit, students see how carbon dioxide bubbled through tap water causes the water to become slightly more acidic, by creating carbonic acid, a weak acid. There are other naturally-occurring gases in the atmosphere, produced by volcanoes and living organisms, that also react with the water in rain to form weak acids. Thus "pure" or "pristine" rainwater has a pH of between 5.6 and 6.0.

The slight acidity of normal rain is actually beneficial. The dilute acid in normal rain leaches or dissolves minerals out of the soil and rocks on which it falls. This mineral-enriched water is absorbed through the root systems of plants, providing them with important nutrients necessary for their growth.

The process of distilling water also makes carbonic acid because of contact between the purified water and carbon dioxide gas in the air, so distilled water is usually also slightly acid, with a pH of about 5.5 or 6.0. This similarity between distilled water and normal rain water is why we suggest that you use distilled water as normal rainwater for the experiments in Sessions 2 and 4.

What is acid rain? Where does it occur?

Acid rain is rain with a pH below 5.6. Sulfuric acid and nitric acid account for ninety-five percent of the acids in acid rain. Sulfuric acid is the type most commonly formed in areas that burn coal for electricity, such as in the Northeastern United States. Nitric acid is more common in areas that have a lot of automobiles and other internal combustion engines, such as the Los Angeles Basin.

There is growing concern over the problem of acid rain, with a downward trend in the pH of the average rainfall (i.e., increasing acidity) in many areas in the United States as well as around the world. The area most affected in the U.S. is the Northeast, where average rainfall is pH 4.0–4.5. Individual storms with a pH as low as 3.0–4.0 are not unusual. Values less than 3.0 have been found. The area in the U.S. with the most rapid *increase* in acid precipitation seems to be the Southeast. West of the Mississippi River is generally somewhat better, except in certain "hot spots," including the Los Angeles Basin, the San Francisco Bay Area, and parts of Colorado. In many other parts of the world, including Canada, the British Isles, Scandinavia, and Germany, rainfall has also become increasingly acidic. Acid rain is a common feature of most large cities.

Is there acid snow?

Though we commonly refer to the problem as acid rain, in fact all forms of precipitation, including snow, sleet, and hail, have shown increasing concentrations of acid. There is even acid fog, which can be particularly acidic. In areas where there is little rain, a phenomenon referred to as *dry deposition* has been observed. Pollutants in dry form fall to the earth and mix with moisture to create acid. The correct term used to describe all of these forms of falling acid is *acid deposition*.

How is acid rain formed?

Acid rain is formed when certain human-made air pollutants travel up into the atmosphere and react with moisture and sunlight to produce acids. These acids dissolve in tiny droplets of water vapor in the clouds and are rained down onto the earth as a solution of water and acid. The reaction by which acid rain is formed takes place in the lowest 10 or 12 kilometers of the atmosphere (the troposphere). The acidity of a particular rainstorm depends partly on how much acid has accumulated in the atmosphere since the last rainstorm. This in turn depends on how much pollution is being produced, and how long it has been since the last rainstorm.

The air pollutants that contribute to the formation of acid rain have long been released by natural processes such as volcanoes, and the activity of soil bacteria and other organisms. However, it has only been with the industrial revolution, including the invention of the internal combustion engine and the extensive use of fossil fuels, that these gaseous pollutants have been produced in great enough amounts to significantly affect the acidity of rain.

Oxides of sulfur and nitrogen are the principal air pollutants contributing to acid rain. These are produced primarily from fossil fuel combustion in power plants, industry, and cars and trucks. Oxides of sulfur (such as SO, SO_2, and SO_3) come mainly from coal burning industry and power plants. SO_x is shorthand for describing the mixture of these three sulfur oxides. Oxides of nitrogen (such as NO and NO_2) come mainly from cars and trucks. NOx is shorthand for describing the mixture of these two gases. Fossil fuel combustion also increases the amount of carbon dioxide in our atmosphere, thereby increasing the amount of carbonic acid formed. However, carbonic acid accounts for less than 5% of the acid in acid rain.

Coal and oil are mostly carbon, but they also have traces of nitrogen and sulfur, which were part of the original plants that produced them. When coal or oil are burned, the carbon is oxidized to carbon dioxide and the nitrogen and sulfur also combine with oxygen in various proportions, producing NO_x and SO_x.

General equations:

SO_x —(combines with oxygen to produce)→ SO_2 (reacts with H_2O) → H_2SO_4 (sulfuric acid)

NO_x —(combines with oxygen to produce) → NO_2 (reacts with H_2O) → HNO_3 (nitric acid)

$CO_2 + H_2O \rightarrow H_2CO_3$ (carbonic acid)

How is acid rain harmful?

There are three major ways that acid rain harms our environment: by contact with plants, by contact with soil and water, and by mobilizing trace metals. The effects of acid rain on plants, soil, and water in turn affect other living organisms that depend on them.

Acid rain can damage plants. Acid rain can harm plants by damaging outer leaf surfaces and by changing the root environment. Acid rain has been found to strip away the waxy protective coating from coniferous needles. Acid rain damage in Germany in the Black Forest includes the death of saplings and "crown droop," the death of limbs at the top of the conifers. Acid rain can keep seeds from germinating. Plants growing in high altitudes (especially cloud forests) are the first to show the effects of acid rain because they are often literally in the clouds, essentially bathed in acid mist.

Acid rain destroys our soil and water resources. We frequently hear about the death of fish or amphibians in acidic lakes or ponds. The water in these lakes can come from direct precipitation into the lake, from runoff water that collects from the nearby soil, or by water from the water table. Because the acidic water permeates their entire environment, aquatic animals are among the first to show ill effects. They act as the "canaries in the mine" to warn us of changes in the acid environment of a lake. Different aquatic organisms have different sensitivities to acid. Even when adult organisms are able to survive in an acid environment, their reproductive cycles might nevertheless be interrupted or impaired. The formation, development, or hatching of eggs, or the development of the young at various stages of growth can all be adversely affected.

Acid rain changes the pH environment of both lake water and the underlying soil (substrate). Many *microorganisms* that form the first link in the food chain have evolved for a specific environment. When the acidity of that environment changes, not only does the amount of hydrogen ions increase, but the change in acidity in turn causes a subsequent change in the nutrients available to these microorganisms. When we change the nutrients available to these basic links in the food chain, we change their population, along with the ecosystem that depends on them for food.

Acid rain can cause minerals in the soil to dissolve too quickly, so they are washed away. While we depend on normal rain to dissolve some of these minerals, acid rain can *deplete* this source of minerals. It takes millions of years to replenish the rocks that supply the parent material for the soil. Many minerals are nutrients for both plants and animals.

Acid rain mobilizes trace metals. Trace metals are metals that are found in trace amounts in the soil or water. When more of these metals dissolve, the amounts in the environment are no longer trace amounts. This may lead to the poisoning (i.e., exposure to toxic levels of nutrients) of living systems. Some metals that have been found in toxic amounts include aluminum, cadmium, lead, mercury, and copper. In the state of Washington there is a problem of aluminum toxicity in forest plants found in acidic soils. These plants absorb excess aluminum, which interferes with their absorption of calcium and magnesium. Magnesium is essential to photosynthesis, for it is an important part of chlorophyll (the green pigment that allows plants to trap light energy from the sun).

Often, wildlife will absorb these trace minerals. This absorption can interfere with the absorption of other necessary mineral nutrients. For example, fish will not be able to absorb calcium and phosphorus in sufficient amounts to allow them to have strong bones. Often, fish in acidic waters have jelly-like bones.

Buffering capacity

Soils and rocks (including those surrounding lakes) often have a natural *buffering capacity*. Buffering capacity is the relative ability of a soil to resist changes in pH. (See previous discussion on buffers in this section.) Hydrologists (scientists who study lakes) sometimes refer to buffering capacity (BC) as *acid neutralizing capacity* (ANC). The greater the buffering capacity a soil has, the more acid is necessary to cause a change in that soil's pH, and consequently to change the pH of the lake formed from water filtering through that soil.

Lakes have their own buffering capacities, different but related to the buffering capacity of the surrounding rocks and/or soil, and influenced by the mixture of chemicals dissolved in the lake water. A soil's pH and its buffering capacity affect the pH of a lake in two ways: 1) a lake's *substrate* (surrounding soil) is in constant contact with lake water; and 2) the runoff water that feeds into a lake often filters through the substrate. However, soil does not always contact runoff, as for instance, when water fails to penetrate frozen or fully-saturated ground, or bare, solid bedrock. Lakes also have other characteristics that can affect their buffering capacity, such as the vegetation and animal life growing in them.

A lake's buffering capacity can be *depleted*. When acidity becomes evident in a lake, this means that the natural buffering capacity of the lake's substrate has been used up to its full extent. When a lake's buffering capacity is exhausted, its pH drops below 6, the lake water can become high in sulfate, aluminum, and other ions, and the amount of life in the lake can be drastically altered and/or reduced. Buffering capacity can also be *renewed*, by such things as the weathering of certain minerals from the lake's surroundings.

How does acid rain affect people?

Although acid rain will not eat through your clothing or dissolve your skin, it affects us at a very basic level. It can affect the quality of the water we need for drinking and washing. It can affect the soil, which we need to grow food to support human life and to build dwellings. Acidity can dissolve trace metals like mercury, aluminum, cadmium, lead, and asbestos in the atmosphere, in the soil, and in water pipes. It can corrode pipes. It erodes buildings and artwork, thus ruining centuries of human construction and expression and constructive work. It dissolves marble statues, eroding away artistic masterpieces.

How is acid rain a global problem?

Acid rain often falls far from its polluting source. Once deposited into the atmosphere, airborne gaseous pollutants are often blown hundreds of miles. Depending on wind speed, direction, and duration, pollutants can stay aloft for four days or longer. Another factor affecting how far the pollutants travel is how high they are deposited in the atmosphere. The tallest smoke stacks can deposit the pollutants high in the atmosphere, where they get carried by the jet stream and other powerful winds.

Canada has a problem with acid rain that is generated in the coal-burning power plants of the Ohio Valley. The acid rain problem in the Black Forest in Germany has been traced to industrial emissions from the British Isles. These facts help us realize that natural forces do not follow state or government boundaries. Policy making becomes especially difficult when the cause of the problem resides in a different country than where the problem makes itself felt.

What is being done to alleviate the problem of acid rain?

A wide variety of solutions to the problem of acid rain have been attempted, with varying levels of success. Some of the solutions address the symptoms of the problem, and others attempt to address the sources of the problem. With each solution, the potential benefits and costs must be weighed. Even once a solution is chosen, ways must be found to fund its implementation.

Building taller smoke stacks. An early (and extremely self-serving) solution sought by industrial polluters was to build taller smoke stacks, so the pollutants could be carried away by winds high in the atmosphere. Sending the pollution elsewhere was a solution from the perspective of industries being confronted by local groups, but it did not address the real issues.

Adding buffer to lakes. Buffer has been added to some of the most adversely affected lakes in upstate New York (in the Adirondacks), in Germany (in the Black Forest), and in Scandinavia. Adding buffer to lakes is sometimes referred to as "liming" lakes, as limestone is the usual buffer used. While liming lakes can raise the pH of lakewater, it does not correct some of the other changes brought about by acid rain, such as high levels of aluminum ions. In addition, liming has to be continued as long as acid rain is being deposited, and the lime itself can have major effects on the ecosystems in and surrounding lakes.

Developing acid-resistant fish. In response to the outcry about depleted fish resources, some scientists have actually worked on developing strains of fish that are resistant to higher levels of acid. This is a good example of a short-sighted solution.

Increasing the use of coal that is naturally low in sulfur compounds. Coal deposits vary in the amounts of residual sulfur they contain. While this solution reduces the SOx emissions, it does not reduce NOx emissions. Also, in the long run, there is often great pressure to return to the use of high-sulfur coal sources after available supplies of low-sulfur coal have run out.

Removing sulfur and nitrogen compounds from fuels and emissions. Scientists have investigated methods of removing compounds that lead to the creation of SO_x and NO_x from fuels (coal, oil, and gasoline) as well as from emissions (from factories, power plants, and vehicles). There have been some successes with this approach, including washing coal to remove sulfur, spraying wet limestone into hot factory exhaust gases, burning fuel at a lower and more even temperature, and reacting coal with steam and air at high temperatures to produce a gas consisting mainly of hydrogen and carbon monoxide. In this last solution the hydrogen gas is burned, causing a turbine to be turned to generate electricity; waste heat generates steam, turning yet another turbine.

However, each of these solutions has its price. Burning fuel at a lower and more even temperature reduces factory efficiency, costing more money and requiring more fuel to be burned in the long run. The solution involving the spraying of limestone only reduces SO_x emissions, not NO_x emissions. It has the further problem of producing solid sulfur waste which creates a difficult disposal problem. The last solution mentioned (where hydrogen gas is burned) causes a plant to operate more efficiently, but it costs a great deal of money to install such a system.

Substituting other energy alternatives for fossil fuels. Hydroelectric, nuclear, solar, and wind power are all energy alternatives that create little or no acid-producing pollutants. Each of these forms of power generation has its costs of installation and maintenance, and its impacts on the environment.

Conserving energy. Expanding the use of mass transit, producing more fuel-efficient cars, driving less, insulating houses against heat loss, and using less electricity are just some of the ways we can conserve energy, thereby reducing the emission of pollutants that cause acid rain.

Part 2: Collecting Soil Samples

Several approaches to collecting soil samples are detailed below, as needed for the activity in Session 4 of this unit. In all cases, collect several handfuls of each type of soil in a large ziplock bag or plastic bucket. Label the bag for future reference, describing where you collected the soil. Try as much as possible to preserve the collecting area, and carefully fill in the small hole your sampling will leave.

The Ideal Way

Ideally, it would be best for you to have soils with a variety of pH's and buffering capacities. This helps demonstrate the natural range of lake acidity, and the range of different effects that acid rain can have on lakes. While you might well arrive at a suitable collection of soils with the easier collection methods described below, you will not be fully assured that the soils you collect will have a range of pH and buffering capacities.

Soils whose pH changes very little after the addition of acid solution are referred to as having a natural buffering capacity. The less the soil's pH changes, the greater its buffering capacity.

It is ironic that soils high in carbonate (buffer) are found in arid regions, places that receive little rain (and, therefore, little acid rain). These soils are high in carbonate because it has not been leached (washed) out of the soil by water.

It would be most advantageous to include a rock-like or granite sample to simulate high mountain lakes with little or no buffering capacity, a soil sample high in carbonate such as limestone to demonstrate soils with a high level of natural buffering capacity, and *several other soils,* such as: rich garden loam, pine forest floor, soil from a burned area, maple woods, oak woods, redwood forest, ocean beach, eucalyptus woods, and so on.

If you do not have access to a forest of a certain kind of tree, get a sample from directly under a tree or small grove of that type of tree. If you live in the prairie, the desert, or in a region with low diversity of environments, a phonecall to your local Soil Conservation Service Office or a conversation with an earth science teacher at your school, or in your school district, should help you locate soil samples of different pH and with high and low buffering capacities.

Soils from burned areas usually have high buffering capacity. If there is not an area near you (forest or grassland) that was burned within the last several months, you can simulate a burned soil. Collect soil from under an older tree and leaf litter from around the tree. Place the soil in your fireplace, scatter the dried litter on top, and burn the litter. Another way to make "homemade burn" is to mix residual wood ash from a fire into a soil. Though not as authentic as they could be, either of these methods will assure a soil that is both quite basic and has a high buffering capacity.

You can quickly test the pH of soil samples while collecting them, using a simplification of the procedure outlined for students in Session 4 of this unit. Shake a teaspoon of soil thoroughly with distilled water, filter the mixture through a coffee filter into a container and test the liquid with a few drops of Universal Indicator solution.

The Easy Way

Perhaps the simplest approach to collecting soil samples for the "Fake Lakes" experiment in Session 4 is to look for dramatic differences in environment. Collect a soil that is affected by a variable, and one that is not affected by that variable. Following are some suggested quick strategies for finding soils of differing pH:

- Soils of different wetness: from a very wet area, from a continuously dry area, and from a somewhat moist area.

- Soils affected by different plants: under perennial plants, under annual plants (collect these two soils at the same measured depth from the surface); soil under a deciduous tree, under a coniferous tree, soil that has no large plants growing on it.

- Soil from beneath a very young tree, soil from beneath an older tree.

- Soil that is under a post or in a yard that neighborhood dogs frequent, soil that is not affected by dog urine.

- Soils affected by human use: in a fertilized field, in a fallow field, in a range land, in an uncultivated field, in an area built on fill transported from another area; soil near a parking lot, garage, or other area where internal combustion engine exhaust would settle.

- Soils on very different slopes: at the apex of a hill, at the backslope, at the toeslope.

- Potting soils, sand from sandboxes, kitty litter, vermiculite from packaging. Call companies listed under "Soils" in the Yellow Pages. They may have different soils or fill dirt available.

Soil Histories

Many of the quick strategies for obtaining different types of soil mentioned above are based on finding soils with a variety of soil histories. A brief summary of how soil histories vary may be helpful to you. Soil histories can differ due to variations in these soil-forming factors: **parent material, climate, organisms, topography**, and **time**. These factors act in concert to form any given soil. To find soils with different pH's, locate distinct variations in these factors.

Parent material is the geologic deposit from which a soil is weathered. Examples of different geologic deposits are: volcanic ash, volcanic rock, deposits of sediments via wind or water, glacial deposits, or bedrock. Soils weathered from different parent material can differ widely in pH. For example, a soil weathered from a sedimentary sandstone rock has a markedly different acidity than a soil weathered from a limestone rock.

Climate refers to the average of cyclical differences in temperature, and the amount and patterns of precipitation. To find soils affected by changes in climatic temperature, look for a soil in an open, sunny field and one under the cool shade of a building or a tree. To find soils subjected to different patterns of precipitation, look for soils on the dry and moist sides of a hill.

Organisms are the people, other animals, and plants that live in and on the soil environment. Organisms add some materials to the soil and take others away from it, thereby cycling nutrients. By cycling nutrients, organisms affect the soil pH. Likewise, organisms are affected by the pH of the soil around them. When looking for samples with different pH's, due to the action of soil organisms, try: soils found under different plants, such as agricultural crops, tree roots, shrubs, grasses, or flowers; soils found in a wild field and soil found in a rangeland, soil in a lawn or park and soil found in an empty lot.

Topography is the lay of the land; how flat or hilly it is. Topography will affect the water table and erosion. A soil at a hill crest will have a different water table than one found in a creek bed or river bed, and so is likely to have a different pH.

Time is how long the soil has been forming, how long it has been undergoing chemical and physical changes. If a soil has been in place for a long time, it will have different properties than one that has been there for less time. An older soil tends to have smaller particles than one that is younger. Check this by looking for differences in the stickiness or plasticity of the soil (and indication of how much clay there is). Often, older soils also have a reddish color. Soils on a shoulder slope have not been in place as long as soils at a toeslope, and so may have different acidities.

Part 3: Diluting More Concentrated Sulfuric Acid to Make a 1 Molar Concentration

If you have sulfuric acid that is more concentrated than 1 molar, use the following procedure to make 1 molar sulfuric acid. **Remember to always add acid to water and always wear goggles when working with acid of 1 molar strength or greater! (Water added to acid can "spit out" dangerously.)**

1. Determine the molarity of the concentrated acid you are diluting by reading the label on the bottle. (Concentrated sulfuric acid is 18 molar. For sulfuric acid, 1 molar concentration is equal to 2 normal concentration.)

2. Put the molarity of the concentrated acid into the following equation and solve for x. (Also see the specific example below.)

$$x = \frac{(100 \text{ mls}) (1 \text{ molar})}{(\text{molarity of the sulfuric acid that you have})}$$

3. The number you get for x is equal to the number of mls of more concentrated acid you should use to make 100 mls of 1 molar sulfuric acid. To do this, measure this number of mls of acid and *add it to* 100 mls minus this amount of distilled water, so that the final total volume of solution is 100 mls.

So, for example, if you have 18 molar sulfuric acid, then you would calculate the following value for x:

$$x = \frac{(100 \text{ mls}) (1 \text{ molar})}{(18 \text{ molar})}$$

$$x = 5.6 \text{ mls}$$

Then you would measure 5.6 mls of 18 molar sulfuric acid and add it to 94.4 mls of distilled water. (94.4 mls = 100 mls - 5.6 mls) This would give you 100 mls of 1 molar sulfuric acid.

4. For each class, you'll need 1 ml of 1 molar sulfuric acid to make 2 liters of acid rain with a pH of approximately 3.0. (The "Getting Ready" section of Session 4 tells you how to prepare the actual "acid rain" solution.) The rest can be kept in a glass bottle as a stock solution. Note: It is generally better to make larger amounts of solution, because the errors in measuring are a smaller part of the volumes measured out, so the concentration is more accurate.

Resources

Reading More About Acid Rain

Acid Rain. United States Environmental Protection Agency, Office of Research and Development, Washington, D.C. 20460. EPA-600/9-79-036. July 1980.

This 35-page pamphlet is an excellent source of easily understood background information. It assumes no prior knowledge of the topic or of chemistry. Though this publication is over ten years old, the information contained in it remains surprisingly current.

"The Challenge of Acid Rain," V.A. Mohnen, *Scientific American*, Volume 259, Number 2, August 1988.

More technical than some, this article is a good source of information about acid rain. It has a particularly excellent and fairly optimistic section on potential solutions to the problem. This includes a projected timetable of reductions in acid-rain-forming pollutants in the United States, keyed to different emission-reducing technologies.

"Liming Fails the Acid Test," Sarah Woodin and Ute Skiba, *New Scientist*, Volume 125, Number 1707, March 10, 1990.

An excellent and up-to-date discussion of the advantages and disadvantages of "liming" (adding calcium carbonate to) lakes, as well as the more recent innovation that involves liming the catchment, or land around lakes. Includes a brief summary of the numbers of acidified lakes treated with lime in Sweden, Norway, Canada, Britain, and the United States. Excellent information on the potential negative effects of catchment liming on plants, animals, and the lake ecosystem, including effects on bird habitats rare plants, and peat moss.

Student Science Projects

The Acid Rain Foundation, 1410 Varsity Drive, Raleigh, North Carolina 27606, (919) 828-9443, publishes a 22-page booklet of experiments, available for $11.95. The booklet includes: experimenting to observe the effects of acid deposition on plants, microorganisms, and different materials; exploring the pH concept and applying it to monitor the acidity of rain and snow; guidance for library study, and related materials. The Acid Rain Foundation publishes a wide variety of other materials, including a quarterly newsletter, curricula for many grade levels, general background information, scientific proceedings, puzzles, and posters. They also provide an excellent listing of audiovisual materials on acid rain, including slides, video cassettes, film and audiotape presentations.

Laboratory Activities in Biological Science, a publication of the Frontiers of Science Project (214 Lyman Hall, Syracuse University, Syracuse, NY 13244-1270) includes, in its Ecology section, a series of suggested experiments to investigate the effect of acid rain on soil bacteria. The introduction says, "There are two purposes for this lab. The first involves developing further experimental designs to produce better results upon which to base your understanding of the effects of acid rain. The second involves extracting experimental data from which interpretations can be made concerning the effects of acid rain on populations of soil bacteria."

Resources on Chemicals and the Environment

The Chemical Education for Public Understanding Program (CEPUP), based at the Lawrence Hall of Science, has developed an activity-based curriculum for use with middle/junior high schools and the public. The curriculum integrates chemical concepts and processes with societal issues in order to develop greater public awareness, knowledge, and understanding about chemicals and how they interact with our lives. Inquiry-based activities emphasize problem solving and decision-making. The CEPUP materials are available from: Addison Wesley Publishing Co., Menlo Park, California; Fisher Scientific Company, Chicago, Illinois; Lab Aids, Inc. Ronkonkoma, New York; Science Kit and Boreal Laboratories, Tonawanda, New York; and Sargent-Welch Scientific Company, Skokie, Illinois.

Contacting the Soil Conservation Service Office in Your County:

There are Soil Conservation Service Offices in every state and every county in the United States. They can help you locate soils of various pH and buffering capacities. Look in the government pages in your phone book to find the office in your county.

Where to Purchase:

Universal Indicator and 1 Molar Sulfuric Acid

Universal Indicator Solution and 1 Molar Sulfuric Acid can be purchased from many different scientific supply companies. If you don't have a favorite, try the following company:

Universal Indicator Color Charts

Flinn Scientific, Inc. also sells Universal Color Indicator Charts very inexpensively. These are otherwise hard to find.

Flinn Scientific, Inc.
P.O. Box 219
131 Flinn Street
Batavia, IL 60510
(708) 879-6900

Sentence Strips

Sentence strips can be purchased from many teacher supply stores. If there's not one convenient to you, they can be ordered by phone or mail from:

Guy's Teacher Supply
5327 Jacuzzi Street
Richmond, CA 94804
(415) 527-0566

Literature Connections

There are a large number of books for young people on the environmental crisis. This list is just a small selection, beginning with several non-fiction works, then branching out to literary connections. We have included a few books for younger children, in case you are adapting parts of the activity for early grades, or if you think your students would enjoy them in connection with the hands-on science activities in this guide. You and your students are likely to have your own favorite books, and we would welcome hearing about them.

Kid Heroes of the Environment: Simple Things Real Kids Are Doing to Save the Earth edited by Catherine Dee, illustrated by Michele Montez. Earth Works Press, Berkeley, California, 1992.

The-life stories of young people who decided to do something constructive about an environmental problem. Provides excellent examples of role models for young and old alike.

Love Canal: My Story by Lois M. Gibbs. State University of New York at Albany Press, 1982. Grades: 6–adult.

Autobiography of the woman who organized a neighborhood association that eventually resulted in a cleanup of the Love Canal toxic waste site and relocation of the families living there. She went on to form the Citizen's Clearinghouse for Hazardous Waste based in Arlington, Virginia.

Our Endangered Planet: Rivers and Lakes by Mary Hoff and Mary M. Rogers. Lerner Publishing, 1991. Grades: 4–adult.

An attractive and user-friendly reference book covering the dangers of surface water pollution. Many illustrations and photographs. Other relevant titles in this series (all published in 1991) include: *Groundwater, Population Growth,* and *Tropical Rain Forests.*

Rachel Carson: Pioneer of Ecology by Kathleen V. Kudlinski. Illustrated by Ted Lewin. Viking Penguin, New York. 1988. Grades: 4–12.

Biography of the influential environmental activist and author of *The Sea Around Us* and *The Silent Spring.* Accounts of Rachel Carson making the difficult decision to be a biology major in college, working to help support her family as a writer at the Bureau of Fisheries (even though she had the highest score on the civil service biologist test), and persevering to have her research and writing published and acknowledged serve as an inspiring example.

Rain of Troubles: The Science and Politics of Acid Rain by Lawrence Pringle. Macmillan, New York. 1988. Grades: 5–adult.

How acid rain was first detected, the way it is transported, and its effects on plant and animal life. Discusses economic and political factors that have delayed societal action. Good background for town meeting component of guide.

And Still the Turtle Watched by Sheila MacGill-Callahan. Illustrated by Barry Moser. Dial, New York. 1991. Grades: K–6.

A turtle carved by Native Americans in a rock on a bluff watches with sadness the changes humans bring over the years. After the rock is cleaned of spray paint and installed indoors at a botanical garden, the turtle's vision is restored and he communicates his wisdom to the many children visiting.

Danny Dunn and the Universal Glue by Jay Williams and Raymond Abrashkin. Illustrated by Paul Sagsoorian. McGraw-Hill, New York. 1977. Grades: 4–9.

Danny and his friends bring evidence to a town meeting that waste from a local factory is polluting the stream. Discussion of societal issues such as tax revenue and jobs that the factory contributes to the town make a good connection to the town meeting in Session 7.

Just A Dream by Chris Van Allsburg. Houghton Mifflin, New York. 1990. Grades: 1–6.

When he has a dream about a future Earth devastated by pollution, Walter begins to understand the importance of taking care of the environment.

One Day in the Tropical Rain Forest by Jean C. George. Illustrated by Gary Allen. Thomas Y. Crowell. New York. 1990. Grades: 4–7.

Takes place just before "doomsday" when a section of rain forest in Venezuela is scheduled to be bulldozed. The young boy, Tepui, works as an assistant to a scientist, Dr. Rivero. They seek a new species of butterfly for a wealthy industrialist who might then preserve the forest.

The Berenstain Bears and the Coughing Catfish by Stan and Jan Berenstain. Random House, New York. 1987. Grades: K–6.

A respected bear scientist helps a wise catfish and the Berenstains to clean up life-threatening pollution in a lake. A sunken treasure chest, some imaginative scientific devices, and the creation of a lake-life museum are part of the story. Although this book has the juvenile humor common to the series, the language level is fairly high and, with a suitable introduction, might be enjoyed by 7th and 8th grades, in connection, for example, with the Acid Rain play.

The Day They Parachuted Cats on Borneo: A Drama of Ecology by Charlotte Pomerantz. Illustrated by Jose Aruego. Young Scott Books/Addison-Wesley, Reading, MA. 1971. Grades: 4–7.

Based on a newspaper article, this cautionary verse explores how spraying for mosquitoes in Borneo eventually affected the entire ecological system, from cockroaches, rats, cats, and geckos, to the river and the farmer. "Parapussycats" are dropped in to eat the surplus of rats resulting from the imbalance. The strong, humorous text would make the book successful as a dramatic reading or skit.

The Earth is Sore: Native Americans on Nature adapted and illustrated by Aline Amon. Atheneum, New York. 1981. Grades: 4–adult.

Collection of poems and songs by Native Americans celebrating the relationship between the earth and all creatures and mourning abuse of the environment. Illustrated with black and white collage prints made from natural materials.

The Great Kapok Tree by Lynne Cherry. Harcourt, Brace, and Jovanovich, New York, 1992. Grades: K–4.

Rainforest creatures plead for the survival of their natural world.

The River by David Bellamy. Illustrated by Jill Dow. Clarkson Potter/Crown, New York. 1988. Grades: 3–5.

How plant and animal life co-exist in a river and their struggle for survival when a man-made catastrophe strikes. Details about stream ecology include a description of the effects of waste water discharged from a factory pipe and how the bacteria, algae, and oxygen interact in the river.

The Talking Earth by Jean C. George. Harper and Row, New York. 1983. Grades: 6–12.

Billy Wind, a Seminole, is known for her curiosity and criticized for doubting the traditional wisdom of her people. Her sister says, "You are too scientific. You are realistic like the white men." Poling through the Florida Everglades sloughs and then a river in a dugout canoe, she fends for herself with an otter, a panther cub, and a turtle as companions and guides. Viewing the destruction after a hurricane, she hears the message of the animal spirits, "we must love the earth or it will look like this... life can be destroyed unless we work at saving it."

Who Really Killed Cock Robin? by Jean C. George. Harper Collins, New York. 1991. Grades: 3–7.

A compelling ecological mystery examines the importance of keeping nature in balance, and provides an inspiring account of a young environmental hero who becomes a scientific detective.

MORE ON THEMES

The word "themes" is used in many different ways in both ordinary usage and in educational circles. In the GEMS series, themes are seen as key recurring ideas that cut across all the scientific disciplines. Themes are bigger than facts, concepts, or theories. They link various theories from many disciplines. They have also been described as "the sap that runs through the curriculum," to convey the sense that they permeate through and arise from the curriculum. By listing the themes that run through a particular GEMS unit on the title page, we hope to assist you in seeing where the unit fits into the "big picture" of science, and how the unit connects to other GEMS units. The theme "Patterns of Change," for example, suggests that the unit or some important part of it exemplifies larger scientific ideas about why, how, and in what ways change takes place, whether it be a chemical reaction or a caterpillar becoming a butterfly. GEMS has selected 10 major themes:

Systems & Interactions	**Scale**
Models & Simulations	**Structure**
Stability	**Energy**
Patterns of Change	**Matter**
Evolution	**Diversity & Unity**

If you are interested in thinking more about themes and the thematic approach to teaching and constructing curriculum, you may wish to obtain a copy of our handbook, *To Build A House: GEMS and the Thematic Approach to Teaching Science.* For more information and an order brochure, write or call GEMS, Lawrence Hall of Science, University of California, Berkeley, CA 94720. (510) 642-7771. **Thanks for your interest in GEMS!**

Summary Outlines

Session 1: Pick Your Brain About Acid Rain

Getting Ready

Several Weeks Before Beginning the Unit:
1. You may want to post a "Coming Soon-Acid Rain" Sign.
2. Students can bring in articles on acid rain.

Before the Day of the Activity
1. Cut paper towels.
2. Cut plastic wrap.
3. Locate appropriate area to set plant growth experiment.
4. Clear space on wall to post butcher paper lists.
5. Label bottles.
6. Make vinegar and water solutions and pour into bottles.
7. Duplicate homework sheets.

On the Day of the Activity
1. Put two cups, two paper towel squares, and two pieces of plastic wrap on a tray for each group of four students.
2. Set up area where students can pour vinegar and water solutions near a sink. Place the vinegar bottle and the vinegar and water solutions there.
3. Put seeds at a seed-counting station.
4. Post several sheets of butcher paper and set a marking pen nearby.
5. Put sentence strips, masking tape, and the rest of the marking pens near the posted butcher paper.
6. Arrange the room so groups of four students can work together.

Pick Your Brain

Introduce the Challenge of the Day
1. Tell the class you want to find out what they've heard about acid rain. Emphasize this need not be correct or complete— anything they've heard.
2. They have three minutes to each write a list of anything they've heard about acid rain.
3. Distribute pieces of blank paper and have them begin.
4. When students run out of things to write, have them turn over their papers and write any questions they have about acid rain.

Organize a "Mind Swap"
1. After most students have slowed down, have them put their pencils down.
2. They will work in teams of four to conduct a "mind swap."
3. Explain the rules: one person shares her list, the others listen and don't interrupt or comment. Students may add things the speaker shared to their own lists. When first person is through sharing, next person begins.
4. Help class divide into groups of four and begin.

Share What Everyone Has "Heard"
1. After about five minutes, stop the mind swap.
2. Call on each group to share one thing they've heard about acid rain. List these on butcher paper.
3. Continue until all information has been shared. It is okay to "pass."
4. Encourage discussion about any two statements that couldn't both be true, and about the nature of "hearsay" information.
5. Tell students they will have chance to refine list as unit progresses and they learn more about acid rain.

Generate Questions: What We Don't Know About Acid Rain
1. Focus on generating questions about acid rain.
2. Explain rules: each group should work together to come up with at least one question per person. To qualify as a question, no one in the group can give an acceptable answer.
3. Ask them to write each question in large print on a sentence strip.
4. Distribute markers, strips of paper, and begin.

Post the Questions
1. After about five minutes, have groups post questions.
2. If you have time, see if anyone can offer a response to any question. Tell them you will return to this list of questions as the unit proceeds.
3. Point out that scientists still have many questions about acid rain.

Healthy Plants or Pickled Beansprouts?

Introduce the Plant Growth Experiment
1. Tell class they will work in groups to investigate whether acid affects plant growth.
2. Show the bottle of vinegar and verify that vinegar is an acid. Explain that they will investigate the effects of various mixtures of vinegar and water on seed germination.

Explain the Experimental Procedure
1. Tell the class that each group will set up two trials: one control trial using tap water, and one a varying solution of vinegar (from 100% to 1%). Explain how you made the vinegar solutions.
2. Show how to label the cups with name of solution, type of seed, and group identification.
3. Show how to line the bottom of each cup with paper towel and add test solution until there is about a quarter of an inch of liquid in the bottom of the cup.
4. Then have them put 10 seeds in the cup and cover with plastic wrap.

5. Tell each group to designate group members to accomplish tasks.
6. Assign each group which vinegar solution and which type of seed to use.
7. When students understand what is to be done, distribute the equipment and have them begin.

Groups Set Up the Germination Trials
1. Check to see that the procedure is being followed.
2. When students finish, have them place the cups in a warm, accessible place.

Introduce the Homework Assignment
1. Explain that in the next session they will focus on what an acid is.
2. In preparation for this, you would like them to find acids in their homes, or in the grocery store, and record them on a homework sheet.
3. Distribute the homework sheets and tell students to complete them by the next class session.

Session 2: Introduction to Acidity and pH

Getting Ready

Several Weeks Before Beginning the Unit
Collect one white styrofoam egg carton for each student to use as a mixing tray.

Before the Day of the Activity
1. Make or purchase Universal Indicator color charts.
2. Label containers.
3. Prepare solutions.
4. Fill labeled squeeze bottles.
5. Duplicate data sheets.
6. Make a long butcher paper pH scale.

On the Day of the Activity
1. Put the labeled cups, one bottle of Universal Indicator Solution, one Universal Indicator color chart, 2 egg cartons, and 2 data sheets on a tray for each group of four students.
2. Fill the labeled cups about one-third-full with the appropriate solution, and put one medicine dropper in each cup.
3. Put safety goggles in central location.
4. Place several drinking straws and two cups half-filled with distilled water near where you will conduct the demonstration.
5. Post butcher paper pH scale on wall.
6. Arrange room so groups of four students can work together.
7. Set up a rinse station if you have no sink in the room.

What's an Acid and How Do You Measure It?

Acids in Your Life: Introduce Acids and Bases
1. Have your students take out their homework sheets. List the acids they found on the board.
2. Define "acid" as the name for a group of chemicals that behave in similar ways. Ask what similarities acids might have.
3. Point out some of the shared properties of acids: taste sour, break up proteins, dissolve metals, conduct electricity.
4. Ask students if they have heard of chemicals called "bases." List several common bases on the board.
5. Explain scientific classification of acids, bases, and neutrals.

Introduce the pH Scale
1. Explain that all acids are not the same strength. Give examples of weak acids and strong acids.
2. Explain that the pH scale indicates how strong or weak an acid is. Ask if students have heard of pH.
3. Refer to the butcher paper pH scale as you explain what the numbers signify.
4. Ask what a substance of pH 7 is. [neutral]

Introduce the Challenge: Investigating Acids and Bases
1. Tell the class they'll be determining the pH of a variety of substances. Introduce Univeral Indicator solution.
2. Review safety guidelines.
3. Demonstrate the procedure:
    a. Put on safety goggles.
    b. Choose solution to test.
    c. Predict pH of solution and record on data sheet.
    d. Use dropper to add small amount of test solution to tray.
    e. Add two drops of Universal Indicator solution and swirl mixture.
    f. Compare color of mixture to colors on pH color chart to determine pH of the test solution.
    g. Record test result on data sheet.
4. Ask if they have questions. Point out that exact amount of test solution is unimportant, but they should use the same amount for each test.
5. When they complete the tests, they should write the names of the test solution along the pH scale on the data sheet.
6. Remind them to be careful and safe in their tests, and to make a prediction before testing each solution.
7. Explain that groups of four will share equipment, but teams of two will conduct experiments.
8. Distribute equipment.

Students Conduct the Tests
1. Have the students begin. Circulate around the room as needed.
2. As groups finish, direct them to "other predictions" list on data sheet and have them predict the pH of these substances.
3. Ask students not to randomly mix chemicals together.

Pool Data from Groups
1. As groups finish, have representatives record data on butcher paper pH scale.
2. Have students set aside equipment so it's not a distraction.
3. Ask why different people might get different results doing the same test on the same chemical. Ask what they think scientists do when they get different results. Explain that data on the chart represents the range of results for each test solution.
4. You may want to ask class how to interpret range of data for each solution.
5. Have class indicate which of the test solutions are acids, bases, or neutrals, and record this on the butcher paper pH scale.
6. Have students share predictions of the pH of other substances. Reveal the generally accepted pH and record this on the butcher paper pH scale.

pH is a Logarithmic Scale
1. Explain that pH is a logarithmic scale.
2. Point out that a substance of pH 6 is ten times more acidic than tap water (pH 7); a substance of pH 5 is one hundred times more acidic than tap water, etc. The same is true for bases.
3. You may want to note these multiples of 10 on the pH scale.

What's the pH of Rain?

The pH of Normal Rain
1. Ask the class why, when they tested the pH of normal rain, it was slightly acidic. While pure water should have a pH of 7, it changes depending on what it contacts.
2. Demonstrate the acidifying effect of air on water:
> a. Add a generous squirt of Universal Indicator solution to one cup of distilled water and ask a student to determine its pH;
> b. Have another student blow through a straw into the water in the other cup for 15 seconds;
> c. Add a squirt of Universal Indicator solution to this cup and have another student determine its pH.
3. Use questions to help students figure out why the water that was blown through became more acidic. [Contact with carbon dioxide.]

4. Explain that this is somewhat similar to what happens when pure water rains down through the sky, mixing with the air as it falls.
5. Point out that normal rain can have a pH as low as 5.6. This slight acidity can play an important and beneficial role. Record the range of normal rain (5.6 to 6.0) on the butcher paper pH chart.

6. Emphasize that though normal rain is slightly acidic, this is not what scientists refer to as acid rain.

The pH Range of Acid Rain
1. Point out that acid rain is rain with a pH of less than 5.6.
2. Explain how acid rain is formed, by a reaction between pollutants, sunlight, and moisture high in the atmosphere, forming acids that dissolve in rain water.
3. Mark the acid rain range of pH 5.6 to pH 2.0 on the class chart.

Neutralization and Buffers
1. Ask what the resulting pH would be if equal amounts of substances of pH 3 and pH 9 are mixed together.
2. Explain that when an acid is mixed with a base, the two substances are said to neutralize each other.
3. You may want to introduce the concept of a buffer. Like bases, buffers alter the pH of acids; they move the pH to a fixed point on the scale. Buffers are used to stabilize pH in solutions.

Session 3: Startling Statements About Acid Rain

Getting Ready

Before the Day of the Activity
1. Make "Startling Statement" signs, one for each student.
2. Duplicate the homework article.

On the Day of the Activity
Re-post the statements and questions from Session 1 and the class pH scale from Session 2.

What Have We Discovered So Far?
1. Refer to the class pH chart as you ask students a brief series of questions helping them to review the concepts presented so far.
2. Ask class to look at statements and questions listed in Session 1 and revise as needed.

The Startling Statements Game

Explain the Rules
1. Tell class they will play a game called "Startling Statements."
    a. Each person wears sign on his back with a question, but does not know what the sign says.
    b. Each person asks five different people to silently read her question, and answer it as best they can.
    c. Record five answers to the question and summarize these answers.
    d. Then, guess what the question is.
    f. After that, they may look at the question.
2. Emphasize that no one will know the answers to all or even most of the questions, so they will need to make their best "guesstimate."

3. Check that students understand what they are to do, hang a question on each student and have them begin.

Analyze the Questions
1. As students complete their poll, remind them to summarize the responses.
2. As most students finish, have them sit down.
3. Question-by-question, students report their summaries to the rest of the class. Invite the class to comment further on what they think the answer is. Then reveal the "Scientific Responses" and some additional information about each question.
4. Take your cues for pacing from the students' interest level.

So, What Have We Learned?
1. Refer to the lists of student statements and questions from Session 1. Ask the students if there are any statements they would like to modify, extend, or add. Any questions they think have been answered? Any new questions?
2. Explain that this process of sorting and re-evaluating information is something that scientists do constantly, and something the class will be doing throughout the unit.

Homework Reading Assignment
1. Distribute the reading assignment.
2. Let the class know they will be holding a town meeting and a good understanding of the information in the article will be needed.
3. Reveal that in the next session they will be conducting an experiment to model the effects of acid rain on lakes.

Session 4: Fake Lakes

Getting Ready

Before the Day of the Activity
1. Label containers.
2. Prepare solutions.
3. Fill labeled squeeze bottles.
4. Acquire soil samples.
5. Prepare coffee filters.
6. Prepare soil samples.
7. Duplicate data sheets.
8. Post butcher paper on wall.
9. Repost class pH scale.

On the Day of the Activity
1. Put four fake lakes, four sheets of white paper, one bottle Universal Indicator solution, one Universal Indicator color chart, one bottle of "normal rain," four rubber bands, and four data sheets on a tray for each group of four students.
2. Set aside bottles of acid rain.

3. Arrange the room so groups of four students can work together.
4. Set up a rinse station if you have no sink in the room.

Discussion of Homework
1. Discuss the homework reading assignment, asking questions that help students review the major concepts covered so far.
2. Conclude the review by noting that burning coal, oil, and gasoline all contribute to acid rain.
3. Refer the class to the diagram in the reading assignment where the oxides of sulfur and nitrogen are mentioned. Review the role of "SO_x" and "NO_x" in the formation of acid rain. You may want to summarize this on the board.
4. Mention that later sessions will focus on solutions to the acid rain problem as students take on roles of different people in a community affected by acid rain.

The Effects of Acid Rain
1. In order to examine solutions, it's necessary to understand the major problems and effects of acid rain.
2. Ask the class to review the major effects of acid rain on humans, plants, building materials, statues, paint finish on cars, and aquatic life. You may want to summarize these on the board.

If You Were a Fish . . .
1. Explain that you will be taking a closer look at lakes, as an example of how acid rain can effect the environment.
2. Ask, "If you were a fish, what pH water would you like to live in?" Help students reason out an appropriate response.
3. Record the safe range for aquatic life (pH 5 through pH 9) on the class pH chart
4. Discuss the effects of non-ideal pH on organisms.

Anatomy of a Lake
1. Ask, "What do we need in order to have a lake?" Draw the elements that students mention. Define the word substrate as the ground and soil that lines the bottom and surrounds a lake.
2. You may want to ask the class to speculate on what influences the pH of a lake and its substrate.

Experimenting with "Fake Lakes"
1. Explain that each pair of students will have two lakes, each with a different substrate.
2. First they will observe the pH of their lake after a "normal" rainstorm, then after an "acid" rainstorm, and then after it has been treated with buffer.
3. Show an example of a "fake lake." Choose a volunteer to help you demonstrate how to set up the lakes:
    a. Remove the coffee filter containing soil from the cup;
    b. Place the cup on a piece of white paper;
    c. Add four drops of Universal Indicator solution to the cup;
    d. Have your partner suspend the filter containing the soil over the cup;

e. Secure the filter paper around the top of the cup with a rubber band;

f. Measure 20 ml of normal rain and pour it over the soil sample. This is the normal rainstorm. Caution students not to poke a hole in the filter paper with a pencil;

g. Determine the pH of the resultant lake by matching the color of the solution in the cup with the pH color chart;

h. Record the pH of the lake after the normal rainstorm, along with soil type, on the data sheet.

Testing Lake pH

1. Ask for predictions as to what will happen to the pH of water as it filters through the soil.
2. Describe the various soil samples they will be testing.
3. Check with students to make sure they understand the procedure.
4. Remind them that the Universal Indicator solution goes directly in the cup, and to be careful not to poke a hole in the filter paper.
5. Remind them of appropriate safety precautions.
6. Explain that each pair will test two lakes; each group of four will share materials.
7. Have the class form groups, distribute equipment, and begin.
8. Circulate among the groups as necessary.

Pooling Data on the Board

1. While students conduct tests, draw a summary data table on a large sheet of butcher paper.
2. As groups finish, they record their data on the chart.
3. Have groups set equipment aside.
4. Ask why different teams testing the same soil type may have gotten different results.
5. Have class help you rank lakes in order from most to least acidic.
6. Ask: Are any of the lakes too acidic for aquatic life to survive comfortably in? Why are some lakes less acidic than others?

An Acid Rainstorm!

1. Have students predict the probable pH value of their lake after being rained on by an acid rainstorm of about pH 3.0.
2. Explain you have made a solution of pH 3.0 sulfuric acid to simulate acid rain.
3. Students will measure 20 ml of acid rain and pour it through their soil sample. They may need to swirl to mix the rain in the lake.
4. Distribute bottles of acid rain to each group and have them begin.
5. When each group has finished, have them record their results on the board.

Reviewing the Data: Effects of Acid Rain
1. Collect the equipment.
2. Set aside two typical lakes of each soil type.
3. Help the class summarize the main effects of the acid rain on lakes with different soil types. Focus on the amount of change that the acid rain caused in the acidity of each kind of lake.
4. Ask if there are any lakes with pH's that would support aquatic life now.
5. Defer the rest of the discussion until the next session.

Treat Your Lake to a Tums®
1. Hold up a package of Tums. Ask what they are used for. Explain that Tums is mostly made of calcium carbonate, a chemical that acts as a buffer.
2. Review what a buffer does. Explain that buffer, just like Tums, is used to treat some acidified lakes.
3. Add one crumbled Tums tablet to one of each type of the lakes you set aside. The other set serves as a control. Tell class they will see the effect of the buffer on these lakes at the beginning of next session.

Session 5

Getting Ready

Before the Day of the Activity
1. Duplicate group descriptions.
2. Duplicate article for homework assignment.

On the Day of the Activity
1. Post results of the "fake lake" experiments.
2. Set out the fake lakes treated with buffer (and the control lakes).
3. Set out germination trials.

Review the "Fake Lakes" and Buffer Results
1. Focus attention on table of results.
2. Ask students to summarize results.
3. Ask if any "lakes" could still support life. What might account for this?
4. Introduce concept of buffering capacity.
5. Focus attention on the fake lakes treated with buffer (and the control lakes).
6. Explain that adding buffer to a lake is an artificial way of attempting to increase a lake's buffering capacity.
7. Have two volunteers determine the pH of each of these lakes and record them on the data chart.
8. Ask if any of the buffer-treated lakes are better able to support life than their control lakes.
9. Help class summarize the effects of the buffer on the fake lakes.
10. Explain that Tums tablets are mostly calcium carbonate and that calcium carbonate is used to treat real acidified lakes.

11. Point out that various buffers are also used to stabilize the pH of aquariums and swimming pools.

12. Ask students to think of possible problems that adding buffer to a lake might cause.

13. Help the class summarize the results of the experiment.

14. If students don't mention the following points, be sure to include:

      a. some lakes are naturally more acidic than others;

      b. some aquatic life can adapt to slightly acid situations;

      c. some lake substrates are more effective at neutralizing acid (buffering) than others.

15. Explain that the fake lakes, or models, show the interacting components of the lake system—rain, soil, and lake water. Scientists often conduct modeling experiments.

16. Ask about limitations of the fake lakes model.

Healthy Plants or Pickled Beansprouts Revisited

1. Focus attention on the seed germination trials. Explain that having analyzed the effects of acid rain on a lake's acidity, it's time to consider its effects on living organisms, starting with plants.

2. Organize class into original experimental groups, count number of seeds germinated in each treatment, determine % germination, record results on board.

3. When all data is on board, as a class, determine the average percent germination.

4. Ask class to interpret results.

5. You may want to further discuss the difference in germination rates, and what the results suggest about the effects of acid rain on plants and animals.

Planning For The Town Meeting

1. Explain there will be an Emergency Town Meeting to discuss the acid rain problem in an imaginary town called Laketown.

2. Students will represent one of four groups in the town meeting: manufacturers, fishing people, politicians, local residents.

3. Read aloud the description of Laketown.

Organize the Interest Groups

1. Tell students they will need to choose the interest group they would most like to be in.

2. Re-read the names of the four groups.

3. Organize the class into these groups, making sure each group has at least several students.

4. Write task list for groups on board: appoint a recorder, a writer, two speakers; read through group descriptions; discuss point of view to present; jot down questions for other groups.

5. Groups spend rest of period on these tasks.

6. Five minutes before end of period, collect notes and questions.

Homework Reading: Solutions to Acid Rain
1. Hand out reading assignment.
2. Ask students to read article and come to class with list of solutions to the problem of acid rain from article or their own ideas.

Session 6: The Salamanders Have Their Say

Getting Ready

Before the Day of the Activity
1. Make large name signs for each character in play.
2. Duplicate copies of the play and the four sample solution sheets.
3. Read and comment on questions turned in by interest groups.

Generating Solutions

Discussing the Homework
1. Ask class for opinions about homework article.
2. Ask them to share ideas of possible solutions.
3. Record suggestions on butcher paper.
4. Remind class of major sources of acid rain. Ask them to summarize how acid rain is formed.
5. Ask for any additional solutions and record.

Why Solutions Are Needed
1. Tell class that solutions they've listed are a good start. Explain that although the problem of acid rain is serious, there is great potential for finding solutions.
2. Ask them to recall some of the serious consequences of acid rain.
3. In order to alleviate the problem, people will need to make an effort to come up with workable solutions. This has begun, but more progress is needed. Sometimes people need to experience the problems more directly before efforts are made to solve them.
4. Students will be presenting a play in which lake animal and plant characters meet to address the problem of acid rain.

Acid Rain: The Play

Introduce the Play
1. Remind class of the physical model they used to learn about the buffering capacity of a lake in the fake lakes experiment.
2. Today they will find out more about the biological part of lake systems.
3. They will visit a lake in their imagination, in "Acid Rain: The Play."

Set Up the Play
1. Some students will be characters; others the audience.
2. Read aloud list of characters with brief description of each.
3. Ask for a volunteer to play each character.
4. Set up "fishbowl" with actors in front center, audience in larger semi-circle around them.

Read and Discuss the Play
1. As narrator, introduce setting of play.
2. Have the actors read through play, reminding them to speak slowly and project.
3. At end of play, ask what they learned. Help bring out the following points:

- It is not only the lake that is affected by acid rain. If some of the organisms who live there are affected, so is the entire ecosystem.

- Plants are at the base of the food chain, so if acid rain affects them, it affects everything.

- Different organisms and different parts of the lake are affected in different ways.

4. Focus discussion on the different roles played by the characters in the play. Ask how these are similar to the attitudes that people sometimes take in groups when there is disagreement on issues.
5. Explain that the main purpose of the town meeting is to look for solutions that appeal to groups with different points of view. Students should avoid falling into the unhelpful attitudes represented by some of the play characters.

Final Planning for the Town Meeting

Organize the Interest Groups
1. Remind class of their appointed jobs in their groups: reader, writer, and presenters.
2. Summarize group tasks on board:
    a. describe group's main point(s) of view
    b. list questions or comments to pose to other groups
    c. generate ideas about possible solutions to acid rain problem that are acceptable to more than one interest group
3. You will return their groups' questions from the previous session along with your comments and suggestions.
4. You will also hand out solution sheets listing sample solutions they might want to consider or modify.
5. Ask if there are any questions, clarify as needed, then begin.

Finalize the Town Meeting Presentations
1. Circulate among the groups to offer suggestions, clarify the circumstances, and help them stay on task.
2. Five minutes before end of session, remind groups that they are to have a clear written statement of who they are, how they view the problem, and what solutions they propose.
3. At end of session, collect each group's statements.
4. There will be several minutes at the beginning of next session to go over what they have prepared and make final changes.

Session 7

Getting Ready

Before the Day of the Activity
1. Read over group statements collected at end of Session 5.
2. You may want to do some extra preparation for the meeting, such as making name cards, banners, etc.

On the Day of the Activity
1. Select and prepare a wall space for posting solution strips.
2. Reorganize room seating into a meeting-like arrangement so groups can see each other and interact.

Introduce the Town Meeting (5 minutes)
1. Introduce yourself as Mayor of Laketown. Give overview of what will happen in meeting.
2. Explain procedure.
   a. Each group has 3 minutes to make statement about who they are and how they see the issue of acid rain.
   b. Immediately following each presentation, other groups will have 2 minutes to ask questions or make comments.
   c. The presenting group will be allowed to make a brief response to these questions and comments (1 minute).
   d. After all presentations, each group will meet again to come up with proposed solutions also acceptable to other groups.

Final Preparation of Group Presentations (5 minutes)
1. Remind the group of what they need to finalize before the meeting begins.
   a. A brief description of who they are and what they do.
   b. A statement of how the issue of acid rain affects them that offers possible solutions.
   c. At least two questions or statements to other groups.
2. Emphasize need for short, strong statements. Groups should avoid unnecessary name-calling or other non-constructive behavior.
3. Have students assemble in town meeting groups. Redistribute their notes from Session 5 and let them begin preparations.
4. Circulate to answer questions, help evaluate and refine points of view.

Student Presentations and Responses (25 minutes)
1. Call meeting to order and state purpose.
2. Call on groups to make presentations, one by one. Help them stick to three minute limit.
3. After each group presents, have them field questions and comments from other groups. Keep these discussions brief.
4. Help clarify points and questions being raised as needed.

Town Meeting: Brainstorming Solutions (10 minutes)
1. Have interest groups meet again to discuss new or revised solutions that address the concerns of more than just their group.
2. Tell groups to write these solutions on strips of paper.
3. Distribute strips of paper and pens.
4. Circulate among groups to help clarify issues and solutions.
5. After about five minutes, have them post solutions on wall.

Acid Rain: The Next Step
1. Adjourn the town meeting. Thank groups for their creative problem solving and promise that as Mayor of Laketown, you will do all that you can to deal with the problem.
2. Ask students to leave the points of view they assumed in the meeting because in the next session they will evaluate solutions from their own point of view.
3. In the next session, the class will also re-consider some of the statements and questions generated on the first day of the unit.

Session 8: "Everything You've Always Wanted to Know About Acid Rain . . ."

Getting Ready

Before the Day of the Activity
Read over the possible solutions students wrote on sentence strips.

On the Day of the Activity
Re-post: list of possible solutions from Session 7, list of questions, and statements begun in Session 1.

Sorting Out Solutions

1. Ask students which solutions they think are best.

2. Invite them to suggest or modify additional solutions that might take into account the concerns of all interest groups. Write these on sentence strips and post them on the list.

3. If you have a large number of solutions posted, help the class narrow the number, by combining or grouping similar solutions.

4. Encourage critical assessment of the proposed solutions by asking questions.

5. After the list of solutions has been honed and discussed, explain that you will conduct a straw poll.

6. Explain the rules for voting: agree strongly (raise both arms and hold your hands together); agree but have some reservations (raise one arm); not sure and want to pass (cross your arms); disagree (thumbs down). Everyone must vote on each solution.

7. Conduct the poll. Summarize the responses to each solution.

8. Explain the importance of individuals in our society learning enough about different viewpoints so they can make up their own minds. Decisions are not "best left to the experts."

9. Point out that a majority vote is not the only way to make decisions, and that there are many ways that issues arise and are resolved.

10. Stress that to be workable, solutions must be based on a good understanding of the problem.

What We Know and Wonder Now

1. Now it's time to see how our understandings of acid rain have changed.

2. Focus attention on the list of statements generated in Session 1 and ask if and how these statements should be further modified.

3. Then focus on list of questions. Which questions were answered or partially answered during the unit? What new questions should be added?

4. You may want to write quotations on the board that emphasize that good questions are at the base of good science.

5. Engage students in a brainstorm of ideas about imagined experiments that could be done to answer questions, or new technologies they could think of to address the problem of acid rain.

6. Reiterate that as information about acid rain grows and changes, so do our questions and ideas for solutions.

7. Encourage the class to keep reading and thinking about acid rain. They may be able to play an important part in helping solve the problem in the future.

100% VINEGAR	UNIVERSAL INDICATOR	LEMON JUICE
100% VINEGAR	UNIVERSAL INDICATOR	LEMON JUICE
20% VINEGAR	UNIVERSAL INDICATOR	LEMON JUICE
20% VINEGAR	UNIVERSAL INDICATOR	LEMON JUICE
5% VINEGAR	UNIVERSAL INDICATOR	LEMON JUICE
5% VINEGAR	UNIVERSAL INDICATOR	LEMON JUICE
1% VINEGAR	UNIVERSAL INDICATOR	LEMON JUICE
1% VINEGAR	UNIVERSAL INDICATOR	LEMON JUICE
WATER	UNIVERSAL INDICATOR	LEMON JUICE
WATER	UNIVERSAL INDICATOR	LEMON JUICE

TAP WATER	BAKING SODA SOLUTION	NORMAL RAIN
TAP WATER	BAKING SODA SOLUTION	NORMAL RAIN
TAP WATER	BAKING SODA SOLUTION	NORMAL RAIN
TAP WATER	BAKING SODA SOLUTION	NORMAL RAIN
TAP WATER	BAKING SODA SOLUTION	NORMAL RAIN
TAP WATER	BAKING SODA SOLUTION	NORMAL RAIN
TAP WATER	BAKING SODA SOLUTION	NORMAL RAIN
TAP WATER	BAKING SODA SOLUTION	NORMAL RAIN
TAP WATER	BAKING SODA SOLUTION	NORMAL RAIN
TAP WATER	BAKING SODA SOLUTION	NORMAL RAIN

VINEGAR	ACID RAIN	NORMAL RAIN
VINEGAR	ACID RAIN	NORMAL RAIN
VINEGAR	ACID RAIN	NORMAL RAIN
VINEGAR	ACID RAIN	NORMAL RAIN
VINEGAR	ACID RAIN	NORMAL RAIN
VINEGAR	ACID RAIN	NORMAL RAIN
VINEGAR	ACID RAIN	NORMAL RAIN
VINEGAR	ACID RAIN	NORMAL RAIN
VINEGAR	ACID RAIN	NORMAL RAIN
VINEGAR	ACID RAIN	NORMAL RAIN